A Cat's Tale

A JOURNEY OF SPIRITUAL DISCOVERY

WILLIAM R. ANGUS

BALBOA.
PRESS

A DIVISION OF HAY HOUSE

Balboa Press books may be ordered through booksellers or by contacting:

Balboa Press
A Division of Hay House
1663 Liberty Drive
Bloomington, IN 47403
www.balboapress.com
1 (877) 407-4847

Print information available on the last page.

ISBN: 978-1-5043-9090-3 (sc)
ISBN: 978-1-5043-9092-7 (hc)
ISBN: 978-1-5043-9091-0 (e)

Library of Congress Control Number: 2017916925

Balboa Press rev. date: 11/21/2017

To: Lynette

I have loved you for eternity.

Frankie

Preface

I HAVE ALWAYS WANTED to write a book. The urge was there, but it was never great enough to spur me on to a conclusion. I never finished my book on Roanoke or my thesis despite all my good intentions. Oh, there were several excuses, but really they lacked validity. This book, however, is different, although like the other two, I didn't write it; this book was presented to me in an extremely vivid dream. The dream did not force me to transcribe it but suggested that I would lose its meaning and direction if I didn't record it immediately, and for that I would be the one to squander inner peace. In the words of *Charlotte Bronte*:

> "I'm just going to write because I cannot help it."

The main character is a charismatic feline by the name of Frankie. He is a tap-dancing cat and is as real as you and I. Our perception of reality is an illusion created by us as we travel through this lifetime. I have chosen to travel the scenic route through life, but of late I have stumbled frequently, and Frankie arrived just in time to lead me back to my scenic path. With his spiritual guidance, I am once again on my way.

Many have asked me why Frankie is a cat and not perhaps a dog. To this I answer, I had no say in the matter, and it is not a question that I would ask Frankie. As Frankie would say, "Cats think, dogs stink."

I have lived with several Zen masters—all of them cats.
—*Eckhart Tolle*

I believe cats to be spirits come to earth.
—*Jules Verne*

Cats are a mysterious kind of folk. There
is more passing in their minds
than we are aware of.
—*Sir Walter Scott*

Someday you might meet Frankie. He is a real charmer. Should he grace you with his tap dancing, be in awe; he is very proud of this accomplishment (more about that later). Frankie is wise beyond his lifetimes, and despite his independent spirit, he appreciates affection and the warmth of a sunlit windowsill. Give him fish, sardines preferably, or milk, and you will have a tap-dancing friend for life. When you finish this book, as I hope you will, remember you are not at the end but at a beginning.

I'm not saying reading this book will make you happier;
fortunately that power resides solely within yourself.
—*Frankie*

There is a reason you are reading this
book; destiny has brought you
to this moment. You are here to further understand,
for goodness and kindness, and I thank you for that.
—*Frankie* 🐾

There is no better means of attainment to the spiritual life
than by continually beginning again.
—*Saint Francis de Sales*

Acknowledgments

No book is a sole creation of an individual author, and in fact, I had very little to do with this one. I need to thank my charming and devoted wife, Lynette, my inspiration, who makes my world such a fantastic place to be. I wish to thank Sam Oosterman, the bright and talented artist who brought Frankie to life in pictures. The images convey so much more than words. Frankie was both honored and flattered to be portrayed by such a gifted artist and wishes to present Sam with a fresh mouse the next time they meet! I wish to acknowledge my proofers and editors: Annette Holmes, Sandra Saunders, Rhonda and Noah Bartholomew, who made my job so much easier. Many thanks go to Brian Garman, a good friend who provided endless technical assistance. I also owe a debt of gratitude to Michele Deluca for her scholarly guidance. Of course, I would be remiss if I didn't thank Frankie, for both his inspiration and friendship everlasting.

CHAPTER 1

Frankie and Lynnie: The Tale Begins

F RANKIE WAS A CAT. A rather short cat who always walked with his tail straight up. It made him feel taller. Shoes would have also worked, but Frankie was short of cash. Oddly, he was always short of cash, but that was okay; for some strange reason, he never seemed to have any pockets. Money, of course, might not have helped anyway, since Frankie would not need one pair of shoes but two, and that could be expensive. In the meantime, he would just have to hold his tail high.

On this particular morning, he was washing up. He licked his paw and then vigorously rubbed his head. He was a self-cleaning kitten, sitting alone in a grassy Manchester park surrounded by a short, black, metal fence. His morning ablutions were abruptly interrupted by a little dark-haired girl with long-flowing ringlets who had come to play. The very girl he was looking for. He had been born to accompany her at the start of her journey. He was to be her spiritual guide.

> Time spent with cats is never wasted.
>
> —Sigmund Freud

I had been told that the training procedure with cats was difficult.
It's not. Mine had me trained in two days.
—*Bill Dana*

I have studied many philosophers and many cats.
The wisdom of cats is infinitely superior.
—*Hippolyte Taine*

Accompanying her was a scooter, rather small, and a soccer ball, rather big. She would kick the ball away but then would go get it. Then she would kick it away again and run after it again. This happened several times. Frankie wished that the young lass would make up her mind. Either keep the damn thing or get rid of it. Try to be more decisive.

Frankie decided to approach the girl, to renew their acquaintance. After all, she did have nice eyes, and nice eyes were a way for Frankie to judge people. Not all people had been kind to Frankie, but despite being a short cat, Frankie could look after himself. After all, once cats had been worshipped as gods. Cats might no longer be so highly regarded, but they were still considered important. There was a cat in Alaska who was the mayor of the small village of Talkeetna, with fans worldwide. You could find him hanging about Nagley's General Store. Although Frankie had never met Stubbs, Frankie, as a cat, was proud to say that Stubbs was a cat. Preposterous? He even had his own Facebook page. Cats were important. Frankie liked to remind people of that.

He approached the little girl. She was taller than he was, but of course she had shoes, a luxury Frankie could not afford. The little girl saw Frankie and shrieked, "Hello, kitty kitty. My name is Lynnie."

Frankie responded, "My name is Frank."

The little, bright-eyed girl only heard, "Meow meow meow meow."

Looking at Frankie, she said, "kitty."

Frankie responded, "It's Frank. Some call me Frankie, but until I know you better, it's Frank. It most certainly is not kitty. I don't call you childie."

Lynnie still only heard, "Meow meow meow."

In frustration, Frankie responded, "Let me be Frank."

The child obviously did not speak feline. She was going to be a lot of work, but this indecisive lass obviously needed help, and Frankie was up to the task. Frankie looked up at the girl and felt he had so much to teach her. Her dark eyes showed that she viewed the world with wonderment, but at the same time, they betrayed an inner knowledge and—there it was!—a spark of recognition. She was young, but there was agelessness in her soft brown eyes.

His mind wandered for a moment as he considered whether she had a small bird in her possession or maybe a mouse. A small mouse would taste good about now, but alas: nothing was forthcoming.

> Who feeds a hungry animal, feeds his own soul.
> —*Charlie Chaplin*

> Before a cat will condescend to treat you as a trusted friend,
> some little token of esteem is needed.
> Like a dish of cream.
> —*T. S. Eliot*

How was he going to communicate with this child and tell her about the wonders of the world? He wanted to tell her that there would be many lonely nights but love would embrace her with open arms when she was ready. In the meantime, love would be a fickle companion. He would tell her that heaven and hell are right here on earth, and luckily she could choose which one she wanted to be in. Money wasn't important, except for shoes. You should live in the now and never let a day go by without doing at least one good turn.

She recognized something in Frankie, and his purrs and meows resonated in her subconscious. They were reunited once more.

For Frankie, it was love at first sight. Lord George Byron and the Brontë sisters loved cats. In this lifetime, Lynnie would become entranced by these authors as she had before. They loved cats, and Lynnie loved them, so how could she not love this little charmer?

> There are two means of refuge from the miseries of life:
> music and cats.
> —*Albert Schweitzer*

Frankie looked up at her, and she said, "kitty?"

Okay, Frankie thought, *I guess I can be kitty for this cute little girl, but she had better deliver some food. Being a philosopher takes a lot out of you.*

She swept him up in her arms and carried him across the road to her home. Frankie, after all, was a charmer, and they were to be friends once more.

It was a modest home not far from Old Trafford, the home of the famous Manchester United soccer club. After some refreshing milk, which did not go unappreciated, she took him to her room. It was tiny, with lots of things that she had collected during her short journey on earth. Quizzically, she approached a teddy bear of approximately Frankie's size and proceeded to strip it of a small Manchester United jersey. The bear didn't appear to mind, but

Frankie did when she put the jersey on him. Frankie approached a wooden, framed, floor-length mirror and thought, *Really? I look like a giant, fuzzy tomato with a tail. This is not going to do at all. I'm a cat. This looks ridiculous. But wait. Where did these little shoes come from?* Two dolls in the corner sat barefoot, looking none too pleased. *They fit. I look taller. I'm super cat, bigger, better, bolder. I can leap tall chairs in a single bound. Let's see Rooney do that. Why, United would be lucky to have me.*

Yes, I was one cool cat. Don't forget: I had a fur coat long before Joe Namath.

Now to life's lessons and the reason we are here, or how Frankie taught an indecisive little girl with beautiful eyes and shoes how this wonderful planet operated.

Happiness, According to Frankie

Now I'm just a short cat—actually I'm much taller than I look—and you may be asking yourself how I could communicate with a little girl who did not speak a word of feline. Like the vast majority of people, Lynnie had forgotten so much on her journey back to this earthly plane, but like any newborn star, in time she would become a brilliant force, shining her warmth over all she met. I had wisdom and a lot of cat, and we were both so very young. But I'm getting ahead of myself.

We cats do not have nine lives. That is just a myth. In fact, we have many more through years of rebirth. Over the eons, we have learned to communicate through our minds. I was once a guest of Cleopatra, a usually nice person, but sometimes she could be a real asp! I spent one life at the Grand Trianon, which was a marvelous residence. I was there at the time of Napoleon Bonaparte and frequently gave him unheeded military advice. I called him Nappie, even though others close to him referred to him as Nabulio, and we were the best of friends, although he was extremely allergic to me. I gave him hives. He would often be seen scratching his chest with his right hand under his shirt. An artist, Jacques-Louis David, painted a picture of him scratching, and the rest is history.

It has been reported that Napoleon had ailurophobia, the fear of cats, but that fear did not extend to me. He even adopted a cat when he was exiled on St. Helena Island. It saddened me when he was exiled. He displayed a real charm. Not all of my lives were spent with famous people—most were of the everyday sort—but make no mistake: they are as important and dear to me as anyone. Unacknowledged people who pass silently through the doors of history can have a huge impact on the world we live in. These silent but saintly souls put forth kindness not for personal glory, gain, or fame but to help lost and in-need souls. You cannot imagine how the smallest kindness, a smile, can radiate out and change the day and, dare I say, life of someone in need. Life is not about taking but giving.

CHAPTER 2

The Wonders of the Universe

CATS FIRST DOMESTICATED HUMANS in ancient Mesopotamia over 100,000 years ago. We have lived side by side with humans through eternity, but unlike humans, we don't forget our past lives. We continuously learn, and we are here to help humans evolve as well. As an aside, dogs live many lives as well, but they can't remember them, and that pretty much explains the primitiveness of dogs. Have you ever seen one chase his or her tail? Or sniff another dog? That can't be pleasant at the best of times. But I digress, and I will now recount how Lynnie and I arrived here and then the rules I offered Lynnie to live by.

There are a number of concepts that humans have trouble with. They are taught that there is one right answer, usually the one that the teacher has in mind, when in reality, there may be several. Humans perceive that there is a start and an end to everything, and yet space is endless. Think about that: if we travelled at any speed, we would never reach the end. If there was an end to space and at the end there was a wall, what then would be on the other side of the wall? Humans view time as linear, always moving forward. But what if time were circular, like a record? Are we living more than one life at a time, separated like the grooves on a record? What if the needle skips? Do we suddenly experience a view from the past? Is this what transpired in 1901 in Versailles (my old stomping grounds) when two respected academics, Anne Moberly and Eleanor Jourdain, claimed to have involuntarily crossed the boundaries of time to 112 years in the past? The world and we are truly a mystery.

Lynnie and I would often sit in the twilight and discuss these mysteries. Even with my past-life knowledge intact, I continue to view the world with fascination. One night on a quiet hillside in Manchester, I was introduced to my first fireflies. As the sun bid us adieu for yet another day, dusk silently crept up the hillside toward us, carrying with it tiny flies that looked like they possessed individual flashlights. As fireflies danced across our night's visage, Lynnie immediately saw the beauty of nature's dance ... I saw food. Oh, there was beauty there, but I still saw food. I am here to tell you that fireflies are neither a hot meal nor tasty. At the very least, I expected spicy. Yet another mystery of life.

We know so little about the workings of the universe, ourselves, and our history. As our knowledge grows, so does our belief and knowledge grow concerning reincarnation. The majority of people in the world believe in reincarnation; it is almost universal in the East. Western society, until recently, has tended to reject the concept, in part because of the perceived lack of reference to reincarnation in the Bible. Others have argued that the Bible was purged of all references to reincarnation in the distant past, as it did not fit the then-popular version of religion. However, in the past few years, there has been a marked shift in the West toward Eastern beliefs.

Lynnie and I once had an in-depth discussion on reincarnation and how it relates to the Bible. We were slowly ambling along a tree-lined boulevard one unusually quiet evening as a warm breeze tickled our faces. Actually, I was doing a modified forward soft shoe shuffle as we walked; a true dancer, after all, must keep in practice to be fit. The gloriousness of the day, its waning brightness and warmth, penetrated to the core of our souls, driving young Lynnie to spiritual thoughts. Ideas coursed through her mind as we walked along in silence, thoughts of our purpose in life that inevitably drew her into an even deeper inner conflict. You see, prior to our meeting in this life, Lynnie had already been introduced to the Catholic faith. She of course trusted her parents and siblings and their provided guidance. We had frequently talked about the wonders of the universe, life's purpose, and reincarnation. Although a good pupil, to Lynnie there appeared to be a conflict between the faith she knew and the spiritual concepts she so dearly believed in. Lynnie was a bit of a rebel in her youth, and she so wanted to believe me. After all, if you can't trust a cat, who can you trust?

That evening, we sat in a flowerbed along the road and watched a beautiful butterfly flit from blossom to blossom. Wayne Dyer beautifully describes his encounter with a Monarch butterfly in his book *Inspiration: Your Ultimate Calling* but for some inexplicable reason fails to inform you not to eat one. Despite being one of the beautiful wonders of the universe, don't eat one. Trust me; you will regret it. The flowers around us were lit up by dancing moonbeams that, while promising a new dawn and sunlight, told the flowers to enjoy the now. Magic was in the air.

So there we sat as Lynnie patted me on the head and questioned how all of what I said fit in with the religion to which she was born. I explained that I didn't go to church. Cats weren't really welcomed since we didn't have pockets and therefore found it difficult to carry change for the collection plate. We could carry change in our mouth, but spitting wet change into the collection plate along with the odd hairball just wasn't considered acceptable behavior. I did get to church once, but I got wacked with a broom. I never knew crackers could taste so good, but apparently you aren't supposed to eat your fill. I still don't understand that. I had thought of bringing a recently deceased mouse as an offering, but humans don't really appreciate the savoriness of a fresh mouse.

So back to the story. I looked at Lynnie and professed that, although I wasn't a churchgoer, I was spiritual, and I had read many biblical passages throughout my many lifetimes, even some religious documents that were never published. You see, as a cat, I'm very curious. I always wanted to know the whys and wherefores, what makes us tick. So with the preface that I wasn't a biblical scholar, just a cool cat who knew a lot about religion, I proceeded to tell Lynnie that the conflict her young mind was experiencing was just a misunderstanding. Here are the thoughts I presented to her one warm spring evening many years ago while sitting in a flowerbed.

CHAPTER 3

Reincarnation and Religion

D IVERSE RELIGIONS THROUGHOUT THE world recognize the belief in reincarnation. It should come as no surprise that one in four Americans believe in reincarnation. Reincarnation is often defined as death of the body when the spirit separates, is judged, and then returns at a later date in a new body. The purpose of reincarnation is to provide enlightenment as we progress to perfection. This process continues until the soul reaches perfection, becoming one with God.

Scholars often point to verses in the Bible as proof of reincarnation. I don't intend to thoroughly argue whether the Bible truly refers to reincarnation; that would require a separate book written by someone far more knowledgeable than me. Look, for goodness sake, I'm a cat. However, if it piques your interest, I have made some observations in appendix A of this book.

We may never have seen a germ, but we know of their existence. Merely, our failure to remember past lives does not invalidate the concept of reincarnation. Nowhere does the Bible reject reincarnation, although it had plenty of opportunity to do so.

So there you have it. People may tell you there is a conflict between organized religion and spirituality, but is there really? Take the word of this cat. Have I ever lied to you? I like to lie around in the sun to absorb vitamin D, but I never lie. I once told a mouse that I was here to serve him, and I did, on toast. Hey, don't knock it until you've tried it. Tastes a lot like chicken.

Children often refer to their life prior to their current life. They will refer to past-life memories that they have retained. They will recall former siblings, parents, and places. Sometimes they will even recall how they passed from their previous life. Some have suggested this is a result of not having been in the spirit world for very long. Of course, Western parents often stifle such talk of past lives in order to prevent their child from appearing weird or out of the norm. Listen to young children; they have insight for us. Our past lives are quickly forgotten as we concentrate on the experiences around us and get caught up in the drama that is life. We forget our past lives in order to experience our current lives without biases so that we can learn the lessons we have selected for this life and follow the paths we have chartered. We must first realize that our bodies are not us but only an outer envelope or covering. Our spirit only resides there for a short time. But here is the important news for you: death does not exist. Life, your consciousness, continues after your shell, your body, ceases to function. Like energy, life continues; it is your form that doesn't. Your spirit is in an everlasting cycle and starts its voyage home. Your self-consciousness, or what some refer to as the monad, is everlasting. It is eternal. You are only dead in this life. This goes to explain why after-death communications are so common when one's bonds are tight and one's consciousness is receptive to another's communication from a different plane.

When you pass, your spirit lives on. It separates from your body, and during separation, it may hover nearby for a short time, watching in minute detail what is happening. People who experience near death often recount what they saw in accurate detail surrounding their body even though they were unconscious at the time. Throughout our lifetimes, we have set triggers when we can return home to the spiritual world if our mission or plan is complete. A trigger may be a serious illness, stroke, or heart attack. These are windows that present to your subconscious the opportunity to determine if your mission on earth is done and enable you to return home. If you are still here and reading this book, your mission on earth is not over. Our brains operate on two levels, the conscious and the subconscious. Access to the subconscious and past lives can be achieved through meditation or hypnosis. The next time you see me lying in the sun, absorbing its warmth, it's not that I'm lazy; I'm meditating and reminiscing about lives past.

The subconscious is a wealth of knowledge and holds our plan for the challenges we are to experience in this life. Access to these plans is difficult, making life's challenges all the more real. After all, the world is our illusion, and in order to achieve the illusion of reality, we must believe. While in our spiritual home, prior to coming to this lifetime, our guides and friends helped us to engineer a plan for our journey that would help us advance or evolve our spirits as we meet predetermined challenges. We may determine who our parents will be and those within our group with whom we will interact. We incarnate in a group, often choosing those who we will come into close contact with in order to resolve issues from past lives. Some spirits just like travelling together and are referred to as soul groups. Issues from past lives often show up in the next. Sometimes trauma to a body, such as an ax blow or wound, will show up as a birth mark in the next life. Or a drowning in one life will show up in the next as an unusual fear of water. Starvation in one life may result in overeating in the next. Sometimes regression can help to eliminate extreme fears once the cause is exposed.

Time between incarnations can vary, depending upon the needs and desires of the spirit. Tibetans call the time between incarnations

"Bardo." It is a time of learning, evaluation, inner peace, awareness, love, enlightenment, and nonjudgment. Near-death experiences often reflect this home between lives. People report experiencing a bright light, being greeted by old friends and loved ones, even pets, especially cats, and basking in love and peace. Many resist their return to their life on earth when told their mission is not completed.

People often ask me, if we can choose being reincarnated into a particular situation, why do we experience pain and sorrow? Do we actually choose sad and difficult life themes? Sorrow and joy go hand in hand, and we learn lessons from both. When people gamble, they search for the elusive joy of winning. It would soon tire if you won every time. If every bet turned in your favor, the initial joy would quickly dissipate. It is the rarity of the win that causes the excitement. If I caught every mouse I saw, I would be one fat cat. It's the excitement of the chase that counts, never knowing if you are about to succeed or lose.

Imagine your life as a book, a story where you are born, learn, always achieve success, and die happily of old age. You never stumble or fail, never run into obstacles; that would be one boring book, not the components of a good story. Would you purchase such a biography? I have had many disappointments, but I know they were put there for a reason, and that is to learn and grow. Your day off is special because it is not the norm. The team you are rooting for winning a world championship is fun because it is not the usual. Teams fail more often than they succeed. True love is so very special because it is not easy to find. You are special because you are here and, whether you know it or not, play an important part in many people's lives, not just your own. We are all intertwined as we proceed through our adventures. We, of course, focus on our lives, but we are only a small part of a much bigger story, one in which we can have positive and negative impact depending on our attitudes and beliefs. There is a purpose, whether you have chosen to be in a drama, comedy, or tragedy. There is an amazing story here. I for one have chosen to take the scenic route through life this time. As you progress through life, your role will keep changing, much as an actor will play many parts during his or her career, and the script is up to you. You will determine how you will influence the world. The director may be God, but you certainly, as a star, have some say in the story. True, our story may have been written prior to our arrival, but we can determine how we act out each chapter, adding adventure and excitement, which a good book needs. You are the main character in the story. Be likeable. Win life's Oscar. We are all here for a reason; hopefully you will play your chosen character well. Upon your arrival on earth, fulfill your purpose and then withdraw to our mutual home.

Shakespeare wrote:

> All the world's a stage, and all the
> men and women merely players.
> —*William Shakespeare*, *As You Like It*, act II, scene VII

Oscar Wilde, of course, had a slightly different perspective:

> The world is a stage, and the play is badly cast.
> —*Oscar Wilde*

The title of our story could easily be *Lynnie's Part in the Play* or *How Lynnie Learned to Act and Really Live.*

I never met William Shakespeare, but friends of mine knew of him. They were not fond of him because he was not a cat fancier. In *Twelfth Night*, Shakespeare refers to caterwauling. Really! We do not caterwaul; our sounds are music to an ear. I could have entertained with my voice if I had not been so taken by tap dancing. When we purr, we send out the seed of comfort to all those within earshot. Then in *Romeo and Juliet*, *Shakespeare* has Romeo state:

And every cat and dog
and every little mouse, and every unworthy thing.

Really! How could he include cats with that lot! Cats also dislike Shakespeare because he was always correcting their English, and that gets a little old after a while. It's also a little-known fact that Shakespeare was a terrible tap dancer.

Never forget, your body is not you. You will be here long after your body has dissolved. We are the fun-loving dolphins, splashing and leaping our way across the universe.

CHAPTER 4
Life's Rules

H ERE NOW ARE THE ten rules to live your life by. Rules that will make your life more fulfilled and happy. Rules that ensured Lynnie's happiness and made those that knew her cherish her acquaintance, and I became one of those.

Rule #1. Don't swallow your hair; hairballs are disgusting.

Rule # 2. Don't trust dogs …

Sorry, wrong list. My hunger and her shoes distracted me. I was wondering what size feet her other dolls have. Sometimes my mind drifts.

Kindness is its own reward.

Here goes:

Rule #1. Be kind to all of God's creatures, especially cats.

One day, I was stretched out on the windowsill enjoying the early rays of morning sunlight when I heard a banshee-like scream. I recognized Lynnie's scream and scampered up the stairs to see her racing to and fro while her brother chased her, dangling a dead spider in his hands. Her brother soon tired of his fun and left snickering while I sidled up to Lynnie to try to comfort and calm her. This was a perfect moment to introduce her to Rule #1. As she wiped the tears from her face and lay on the bed, I cuddled up to her and started to explain that all living things on this earth are creatures of God and are not to be feared. Yes, we have to take certain precautions if we encroach on certain creature's territory, but in general, all creatures are just doing what they need to do to survive. A spider (at least in the north of England) is not a harmful creature to humans and can be admired for its skill to exist in this cluttered world of giant proportions, from a spider's perspective. We spoke of the oneness of the world and how we are all meant to coexist and help each other wherever possible. A spider may not be something you want in your bedroom; however, you could coax it into the wall where it came from or gently put it outside where it can exist without troubling you.

Lynnie once asked, "Why are there animals?" I responded, "Why are there humans?" In many ways, our lot in life is still a mystery to most of us. I often wonder why cats are so smart and cute. We all have a purpose here. I am a life guide. I sometimes think animals like humans more than humans like animals. There are numerous accounts of animals rescuing humans. There are many verified stories of dolphins saving humans about to be attacked by sharks. Although dolphins can kill sharks by ramming them, they are rarely violent to humans. They have formed protective rings around endangered swimmers to guard them. That is exactly what happened off the coast of New Zealand in 2004. They have also lifted drowning swimmers to the water's surface. Such accounts have proliferated from far-apart places such as Australia, the Red Sea, Alaska, and the many seas in between. Sea legends of dolphins saving humans and whales abound.

I would be remiss if I didn't mention we cats also have been known to rescue endangered individuals. A seven-year-old Bengal cat, who went by the name Simba, saved a Suffolk family when a fire alarm proved faulty. Cats have been known to fend off dangerous predators in order to protect their owners or to help them when they have fallen ill. Like Lassie, if you stumble, we'll be there. And I have to give credit here to dogs who have protected and saved humans many times.

We all share this planet and are here to learn. I have always judged people on how they treat animals, and in particular cats.

> I am fond of pigs. Dogs look up to us. Cats look down on us.
> Pigs treat us as equals.
> —*Winston Churchill*

Animals possess unwavering love for you. Their hearts are open, their minds nonjudgmental. They don't care if you are overweight or lack the beauty standards imposed by society. Lions love you too, but they view you more as food. What possible reason could there be to hurt one of us non-lions? We are here to inhabit this planet and to interact with each other. I'm not going to push karma, but random acts of kindness do multiply, and I always get a warm feeling when I do something nice without expectation of return. Try it; it will make you feel good, and frankly, it makes me want to purr.

Why not make people happy if you can? It takes very little effort, and an act of kindness today just might make someone else's day. And hey, if you get a saucer of milk, consider it a bonus.

Notice the world around you. Your smile or helping hand might make all the difference to one of your fellow travelers in this world. Thank someone for doing a good job or service for you. Thank-you notes generally have a nice impact on people. It really takes so little to give warmth and a spiritual lift to others. John Kralik explains in his book *A Simple Act of Gratitude* how he sent 365 thank-you notes over the course of a year, and it turned his whole life around.

Some may object to your overtures, but do not judge them, for we really do not know what causes or influences their actions. Some people may be so negative that as a last resort, it may be the best course of action to just avoid them. Their negativity, like an illness, could spread to you if you are not careful. Think good thoughts toward them, send them the light of kindness, and let them go their way. Some people just choose to live in a dark world full of woe. Feel sorry for them, for theirs is not a good life. They fail to see the beauty within themselves.

Kindness and goodness create more kindness, as those receiving it, in many instances, will be inspired to help others. Acts of kindness, of course, will make you feel good, the recipient feel good, and, depending on your religion, your maker smile down on you. In your future, make the world a better place. The smile is a universally understood communication of friendship, except for dogs. What is with these dogs? Dogs when they get angry show their teeth. When you smile at a strange dog, you show your teeth, which to them is a challenge. I never smile at a dog. I merely start tap dancing away. A tap-dancing cat totally bewilders them, and I easily make my escape.

Happiness and being kind are contagious. You can be a carrier of goodwill.

> It is one of the most beautiful compensations
> of this life that no man
> can sincerely try to help another without helping himself.
> —Ralph Waldo Emerson

Your random acts of kindness will flow from you like ripples on a pond, hit the far shore, and rush back to you, causing betterment in the world with unasked-for rewards for you. After trying one good deed a day, go for two or three. It's easy and will soon become second nature. Many rewards will be yours. If every day each entity who inhabits this planet did one good deed as simple as opening a door for someone, helping someone clear a walkway, or merely sending the warmth of a smile to a stranger, what would this planet be like? There are so many people who need to be acknowledged or shown care for. A simple thank you might suffice to ensure the happiness of their day; it could even change their life. They merely need your acknowledgment, your approval, and your love.

You see, kindness costs nothing; it can be freely given. That is why we are here. For those of us who are fortunate enough to have done well in this life, we have been given the tools to help others. In helping them, you will be helping yourself. I cannot begin to describe the joy and inner warmth I feel when I can bring joy to others. As sung by the band Three Dog Night, "Joy to the World." You sometimes just have to forgive the use of the word dog.

> I've learned that people will forget what you said,
> people will forget what you did,
> but people will never forget how you made them feel.
> —*Maya Angelou*

> Nothing in this world is more important than love,
> shoes may be a close second,
> but love is the sunlight that warms the core of our soul.
> —*Frankie* 🐾

Don't do good deeds because you want good returns. Do them because it is the right thing to do, and as sure as a cat will land on its feet, good things will be yours. Perhaps because we cats always try to do good deeds, people say things like "cats always land on their feet," "cool cat," "cats have nine lives," or the common "cat's eye," which refers to a precious gem. Of course, not just our eyes are precious; we are precious all over. We are the cat's meow. But once again I digress. Good things really do happen to those whose spirit truly loves their existence and those around them.

When you are a kind person, you gain people's trust, your body releases endorphins that will make you feel good, and hence you will experience a rise in happiness. If you meet someone who dislikes you, and for which there is no method that can create a friendship, then practice avoidance. You may even run into cruel people; unfortunately there are lots of them. They really don't enjoy their time here, and their only joy may be in making your stay worse than theirs. These are the people who hate everything, particularly people who are not like them. Have compassion for them. Their life is a misery where fleeting joy is secured at the expense and hurt of others. I call these individuals toxic people. I have met many a dog where avoidance was necessary. Not everyone will like you or understand you, and that is okay. It will be their loss. Send them love and be on your way. Otherwise you will only end up fighting like cats and dogs, and that will help no one. It's better to let sleeping dogs lie.

Choose being kind over being right and you'll be right every time.
—*Richard Carlson*

CHAPTER 5
Go with the Flow

R ULE #2. NEVER REGRET a decision once made; learn from your mistakes.

One evening, Lynnie returned from school looking a little tuckered out as she put her books on her bedroom desk. She sat in her chair unmoving and silently staring at the textbooks before her, almost trance like. I rubbed up against her leg to let her know I was there to support her and inquired why she was not her usual jovial self. It had been a long day for her, and she still had a writing assignment to complete, dealing with a historical figure who changed history by making an unexpected decision. *Oh, this will be fun*, I thought. I loved to relate stories of my past, and I cherished an audience. So we put on a Herman and the Hermits album to get us in a relaxed mood, and I told Lynnie to sit back, relax, and I would relate to her one of my adventures on a small, insignificant hill long, long ago on the other side of the ocean.

It was July 2, 1863, a month and day that would become important in Lynnie's life almost a century later. I was lazily walking through dense underbrush on a wooded, hilly area looking for a bit of lunch. Despite the tranquil setting, I had heard a lot of unusual noise over the past two days. Horses, wagons, and men were on the march. I felt I might discover some nourishment or generous handout around a friendly campfire. After all, I kept mice away, and there might be a reward given to such a skillful and accomplished hunter. I found myself that day on Little Round Top in a small hamlet named Gettysburg in southern Pennsylvania. As I moved out from under a bush, I came face-to-face with a full-mustached colonel who was discussing a dire situation. After a quick glance at me, he returned to the urgency at hand. The 20th Maine troops were out of bullets, and the seasoned Alabamians where down the hill a short distance away, hoping to outflank the Union line. Normally, when ammunition runs low, you withdraw from the conflict, but Chamberlain was new to battle strategy and knew that withdrawal could likely cause the collapse of the Union line. His troops anchored the line, and he felt a duty to maintain it. Having spent many years with Napoleon, I knew a little about military strategy, but Chamberlain did the unexpected. He ordered his men to fix bayonets. This initially caused me more than a little concern and surprise. Sometimes mistakes aren't really mistakes, and I began to see the wisdom of his plan. Sometimes the solution is the unexpected.

As he walked behind his line of soldiers with saber drawn, yelling preparation orders above the din of the battlefield, our eyes met. I knew that this soldier without strategic military training was about to do what military historians would categorize as a foolhardy mistake. I knew that you should never regret a decision once made, as it is part of your journey forward. I'm sure he must have momentarily wondered what a cat, a rather handsome cat, was doing there on his hillside. I winked at him to let him know I supported his decision. The sound of cannon fire tore him away from our chance meeting, and he hurried along the line. A moment later, I witnessed him charging down the hill toward the Confederate line and into the pages of history. Colonel Chamberlain had ordered a charge without bullets and routed the enemy, saving the Union line and perhaps the war for the North.

I was in full swing relating past lessons I had been gifted with, so I told Lynnie another story that occurred years later. I had met a young man who wanted to get a good education but was as yet unaware of the career he wanted in life. He had entered law school and had immediately taken a dislike to the individuals who made up the profession. He wanted to quit, but that would suggest failure to his acquaintances, and his pride would not allow the unfair mantle of failure to be placed upon him. He worked on tirelessly and disgruntled for the next five years, all the while regretting his choice of profession. What appeared to him at first as a momentous mistake turned out to be one of the best decisions he would ever make. His law degree and subsequent call to the bar had changed his thought patterns and sharpened his mind, opening numerous doors and opportunities for him for the rest of his life. Again, I must emphasize that what are thought of as errors in judgment, in reality, are not that at all. This was to be a life-changing event, a decision that would eventually lead to his meeting with Lynnie. Unbeknownst to him, what he considered a mistake would eventually lead him to the adventure of a lifetime and the love of his life. Once again, I'm getting ahead of myself. There is so much that I want to tell you before I return home.

Lynnie, like me, had a fondness for Napoleon. She had never met him as I had, but I would regale her with stories about him. My vanity made me conscious about my height. I needn't be tall in every lifetime, but once would be nice. You see, I am not a perfect cat. I also learned a lot from my association with people, particularly Lynnie. Where was I going with this? Oh yes, I was relating to Lynnie that Nappie liked to have tall guards around him. I told him this was a mistake, as it gave the illusion that he was short, a subject I was well versed in. When Nappie passed, it was reported that he was 5'2", but these were French units. In English units, this would make him just shy of 5'7". Keep in mind that in 1821 the average male height was 5'5", thus making Napoleon taller than the average man of his time. The nickname, "The Little Corporal," may not have been accurate, but it furthered his fame, and whereas history has forgotten me, Nappie will forever live on.

Sometimes perceived mistakes aren't in reality mistakes. I remember one late night discussing with Nappie the problems of communicating in the dark. I have great night vision. Unfortunately, soldiers do not. We discussed night communications and came up with night writing, raised symbols that would enable soldiers to communicate at night without the use of light and without making any sound. It proved too difficult for the soldiers to utilize and fell into disuse. A mistake? A young blind boy later adopted night reading. His name was Louis Braille, who developed the Braille system for those with poor eyesight. Napoleon's idea, if a mistake, was a brilliant one indeed.

Pope Gregory IX in the thirteenth century had it in for us cats and told his followers in his Bull Vox in Rama, "The evil black cat had fallen from the clouds bringing unhappiness to man." He even connected cats with devil worship. This just wasn't us, but we were killed in droves throughout Europe. Our mass extinction caused the rat population to explode, carrying with it the bubonic plague, resulting in the death of millions of innocent people. This was truly a mistake of gigantic proportions, but still, lessons were learned. Stupidity is making the same mistake over and over. The smart person learns from each and every mistake.

If you really don't want that soccer ball, just kick it away. If it comes back to you because you hit the goal post, kick it again and consider yourself lucky because you are probably playing for Chelsea. Each decision moves you along your life's path to an ultimate goal—your life goal. Each step you take to the right or left, forward or backward, carries you to your current future. It made you what you are today.

You cannot change your past, no matter how hard you try, but you can change your future.

> I am not a product of my circumstances,
> I am a product of my decisions.
> —*Stephen Covey*

> You can never regret anything you do in life.
> You kind of have to learn the lesson from
> whatever the experience is
> and take it with you on your journey forward.
> —*Aubrey O'Day*

You have charted your route before birth, but that doesn't mean that you don't have free will. You can deviate from your chosen path if you so choose. The opportunity is there to be or do anything that you desire. The only criterion is that you have to believe. We are not just talking about hoping something will happen but truly believing it will.

Talk to someone who has achieved something great and ask them if they ever thought this could happen. Henry Ford once said, "If you believe you can or you believe you can't, you're right." How could you ever achieve anything if you believe that you won't succeed? Do you want to hire an employee who thinks you can't succeed or one that thinks you can? The former has already accepted failure. Thomas Edison did not succeed in numerous attempts at creating a functional lightbulb. In fact, Thomas knew ten thousand ways not to make a lightbulb. Yet Thomas believed in himself and endured. Otherwise I would sometimes be drinking my milk in the dark.

> I've never made a mistake.
> I've only learned from experience.
> —*Thomas Edison*

The word *mistake* connotes a negative meaning. It is defined as wrong, misguided judgment, omission, goof, slip, or as my friend Nappie would say, a faux pas. When I first arrived in France at the Grand Trianon and met my newest pupil, Napoleon Bonaparte, he often used the expression *faux pas*. Unfamiliar with basic French, I thought he was saying "for paws" and immediately felt, as I was the only one in the room with paws, that he had something for me. I'd get all excited, anticipating food but to no avail.

We assume mistakes are a bad thing, but are they really? Sure if we make the same mistake over and over again, that is not a good thing; in fact, it borders on insanity. But what if we learn from our mistakes? A baby learns to walk by attempting and failing multiple times until it learns to stand on its own two wobbly feet. From each attempt and failure, the child learns something and is a step closer to its goal of walking steadily. Luckily, when I last mastered the ability to walk, I was already very close to the ground. Mistakes tell us what doesn't work, perhaps pointing us in a new direction. Never be afraid to fail. The Wright brothers failed numerous times, but they followed their dream, learned from their mistakes, persevered, and flew into the storied history of aviation. I would be more concerned if I never made a mistake because that would indicate that I am either doing nothing or perhaps dead.

As I mentioned, mistakes are invaluable. They teach us lessons from which we can learn a great deal. None of us are perfect. Embrace your mistakes. The Wright brothers failed. Edison failed. What makes you any different?

> I've failed over and over and over again in my life
> and that is why I succeed.
> —*Michael Jordan*

The mistake presents you with the gift of knowledge. Accept the gift and move on. Successful people do. Some people fear that they will be thought less of or even laughed at because of their perceived error. Mistakes and stupidity are not synonyms. In fact, the Japanese view mistakes as a step in the learning process, efforts that enable us to grow and learn to solve problems.

> Anyone who has never made a mistake
> has never tried anything new.
> —*Albert Einstein*

Admit your mistakes, learn, organize your thoughts, and move forward.

> Mistakes are a part of being human.
> Appreciate your mistakes for what they are:
> precious life lessons that can only be learned the hard way.
> Unless it's a fatal mistake, which at least,
> others can learn from.
> —*Al Franken*, Oh, the Things I Know, 2002

Mistakes should be viewed as positives, helping us to learn and move forward. Let's call mistakes life's lessons or indicators of advancement. They need not be viewed as negatives.

> The man who makes no mistakes does not usually make anything.
> —*William Connor Magee*

> Don't argue for other people's weaknesses.
> Don't argue for your own.
> When you make a mistake, admit it,
> correct it, and learn from it.
> —*Stephen Covey*

> Mistakes are the portals of discovery.
> —*James Joyce*

I once heard of a company that ran a campaign entitled "Do it right the first time," stressing that mistakes were bad. I knew of another company that actually gave an annual award for what they classified as the best mistake—a mistake where something didn't actually work, but it was a great idea at first glance. Which company, in this extremely competitive global economy, do you think had the most creative employees? Stressing the need to eliminate all mistakes will paralyze your employees with fear. You mustn't make the reward for doing nothing greater than that for attempting to improve; otherwise the world will quickly pass you by and you will be relegated to oblivion.

> Laughing at our mistakes can lengthen our own life.
> Laughing at someone else's can shorten it.
> —*Cullen Hightower*

Try things, learn what works and what doesn't, and then go forward and achieve your dreams. Lose your fear of mistakes and enjoy the adventure of discovery. For years, humankind couldn't fly because we knew it couldn't be done, and then someone said, "Why not?" All it took was the thought of possibility to ignite our imagination and achieve the heretofore impossible.

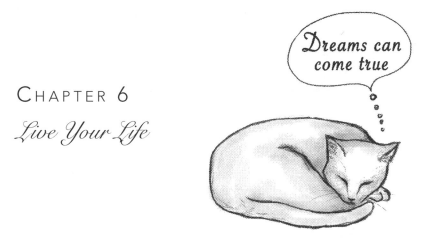

Dreams can come true

CHAPTER 6
Live Your Life

R ULE #3. MAKE YOUR dreams a reality.

As Lynnie was growing, I noticed a shyness and lack of confidence creeping in. I haven't had to traverse this earth as a human, but I was aware that as you move out into the world and your experiences grow, a human can either go boldly forth or retreat somewhat in fear of failure. I was afraid that Lynnie was losing some of her spontaneity and the joyfulness that was innate within her. She was isolating more and living in her own little world in the safety of her home and mind. I knew she was destined for much bigger things and wanted to try to instill some confidence in her, so I took this opportunity to teach her about the power of her thoughts and dreams. When you combine thinking with actually feeling that your dreams come true, the implementation comes naturally, and confidence flows like the mighty Niagara River, fast and furious. Lynnie would someday live by the Niagara River, but she had no idea what the world had in store for her at this moment in time.

You can be a part of the play or merely a member of the audience. Be a participant in life, not an observer. Never envy others or the role they play. We each have different parts to play. Having a dream is a good thing. *Walt Disney* once said, "If you can dream it, you can do it." What a fantastic thought. If you want it, go get it. The key is that if you dream it, then go and achieve it. Otherwise, all you will have is a dream, and as you grow older, you will have earned regrets. Wayne Gretzky had great hockey talent at an early age and a dream to play in the NHL. Achieving his dream took hours, days, months, and years of practice. Hard work enabled his dream to come true. Without the hard work and a belief in himself, his dream would have just remained a dream.

> *You are never given a wish without also*
> *being given the power to make it true.*
> *You may have to work for it, however.*
> —*Richard Bach*, Illusions: The Adventures
> *of a Reluctant Messiah,* p. 120

I once knew a woman entrepreneur who while becoming a bored housewife decided to change her life and start her own business. She had no business knowledge, but she did have incredible belief in her business and skills, and her company grew overnight to employ thousands. One day, I was accompanying her and a reporter through a brand-new facility designed like a Spanish villa. It was truly magnificent. She had just won a national award as the year's top entrepreneur. The reporter looked at her and asked, "In your wildest dreams, did you ever think it would come to this?" Her curt response was a short, "Of course."

Nothing is worse than to reach old age and look back on your life with regret, wishing you had become a professional or finished a degree or travelled to a distant land. It's never too late. Sure, the sports career may now be out of reach because of elevated age, but you could still be involved in professional sports in another capacity. Find what you love and do it. The old adage is so true; find what you love to do, and you will never have to work another day in your life. That's my philosophy, and as a result, I have been travelling the scenic route through life. I enjoy what I do—and why not? Work is fun, or it can be. It's really up to you. Who says work has to be hard and a struggle? Who made fun work an oxymoron? I have no plans to retire. I plan on being busy until it's time for me to go home.

Don't put things off. Time won't wait for you. Don't grow old and wish you had done something or tried something. "Don't die with your music still in you," *Wayne Dyer* said. Every great athlete knew that someday they would be a superstar and worked hard for it. Merely wishing will not make it happen. Sure there are some things that you just can't become. For instance, I will never be a horse no matter how hard I try. Sure I could walk like a horse, swish my tail, and gallop, but people would just say I was horsing around.

> The mind is everything. What you think you become.
> —*Buddha*

> The only person you are destined to become
> is the person you decide to be.
> —*Ralph Waldo Emerson*

> You become what you believe.
> —*Oprah Winfrey*

A dream needs a plan to become reality. To have a dream come true, you must first have a dream. What is it you want in life? What experiences do you desire? What do you like to do? What is your goal in life? Visualize your future success. Many athletes use visualization as a means to improve their game. Basketball players may visualize scoring baskets while going about their daily routine and often credit their success to this method, as did one Canadian Olympic team.

Perhaps creating a dream journal would work for you. Establish some goals, markers along the road to your dream. Travel forward, leaving the past where it belongs, in the past. Look forward to the future. Dreams that do not come true will only remain as wishes. These you can achieve merely by throwing coins in a fountain. Did you really expect that to work? Don't just blow out the birthday cake candles and make a wish; get it done.

Of course strategies need to be reviewed and revised often. Opportunities and inputs have a habit of changing regularly, so you will need to be flexible. Even your dream may change. You may have to make sacrifices to achieve your dreams. You may have to delay doing things you truly love to do or postpone them. There is only so much time in a day, and catnaps may have to be fewer if your dream is to become a reality. A review on how you currently spend your time may be helpful. Perhaps a little less television time or partying will provide the time necessary for you to work toward your dream. Prioritize, and if something is holding you back from achieving your dream, overcome it. Make choices that will help deliver your dreams. Excuses are not an answer. Nothing is impossible. Let your dreams progress down the tracks to your future and don't let everyday life problems derail your destiny.

Once you determine your dream, believe in it and remain confident. Lots of people will tell why it can't be done, one of whom may even be you. Turn them away and believe your dream is materializing, maybe slowly but materializing before you. Don't be waylaid by negatives or procrastination. Don't lose hope if success isn't immediate. It wasn't for the Edisons, Einsteins, or Wright brothers of this world. Bumps may occur along the road, but they can be overcome. Close the door to fear and move forward. Once more, remember to create a strategy with a step-by-step plan. I learned a lot of strategy from Napoleon, and when I set out to do something, I often create a plan. What if the mouse goes right or what if he goes left? What things may help me or hinder me? What are all the possibilities? Lunch can sometimes be tricky.

Now really live your dreams. Once you achieve them, create new dreams. May many exciting days lie ahead. Aladdin's lamp had a genie who made dreams come true. You can be your own genie. Live the life you have always imagined. A new day awaits you.

Be what you can be. There are an unlimited number of possibilities, and several are just right for you. Ever thought you would be reading a book written by a cat? Well you are now. Believe, change your thinking, dream, and watch it happen.

CHAPTER 7

You Are Impervious to Hurt and Pain

R ULE #4. NO ONE can hurt you or let you down.

Lynnie looked dejected and threw her coat on the bed as she proceeded to slump down in a nearby chair. I could not help but feel for this young girl with the expression that clearly showed hurt and sadness. The neighbor boys did not want her to play soccer with them, and the older siblings did not want a young kid hanging around them. Considering myself very observant, I was surprised to find that I had been unaware that there was a young goat living in the neighborhood. Lynnie explained to me that kid was slang for a young child. I asked if wasting her time worrying would help. She responded that they had hurt her feelings and that was not right— she was a good person. I countered with, "What they did was wrong, but you brought forth the hurt. You are allowing yourself to respond in this manner." I then told her my rat joke to lighten the mood. It goes, how do you catch a rat? First you dig a deep hole and then put ashes in the bottom of it. Around the rim of the hole, you place peas. When the rat comes to have a pea, you kick him in the ash hole. With that we both started to laugh, and Lynnie threw a pillow at me, which I deftly avoided. I suggested we go for a walk and leave the hurt behind, and with that, we headed to the stairs. Later that night, I chewed a hole in the neighbor's soccer ball. After all, I'm not perfect, but life was good once again.

Not too long later, sadness attached to Lynnie once more. Lynnie was sitting watching TV and not paying much attention to me, even though this was our usual time to cuddle and for me to show her my best purr possible. She was looking at the TV, yet her eyes were glazed, and I could tell she was somewhere else and not present with me and the family. I nuzzled and nuzzled, trying to get her attention, until she eventually looked at me and gave me a forced smile. I communicated to her that maybe we should go for a walk, and she acquiesced, obviously not into what she was watching on TV.

We talked as we meandered, and she confided that a girl who she thought was a friend had been saying untrue and nasty things about her in school. Although her best friend told her not to worry, she was still upset that someone could be so mean and she struggled with the question, why? I knew this was a human rite of passage, and for some unfathomable reason, people did this to one another to make themselves feel better. Never could figure that one out. I guess it's like a bully who needs to make someone else feel inferior through physical or verbal dominance in order to get a feeling of superiority. This was a big lesson, and one that she would be faced with periodically throughout her life, so I knew my words had to be chosen well.

I knew she had read of Eleanor Roosevelt in her school studies, so I used a quote from her to start:

> No one can make you feel inferior without your consent.
> —*Eleanor Roosevelt*, *This Is My Story*

She thought about this for a moment and then, puzzled, said, "But I never said or did any of the things she accused me of." I then reminded her of Don Miguel Ruiz's second and third agreements: Don't take things personally, and don't make assumptions. I explained that most of the time when someone is accusing you of something untrue, the problem is not yours but theirs. They very often are projecting a problem they have onto you because they are not willing to own it yet. When Lynnie heard those things, she probably assumed that the "friend" wanted to make her feel bad, but the truth is more likely to be that she needed to boost herself up for some reason, or she didn't like the fact that Lynnie came first in the class exams, or some other reason. It was about *her*, not about Lynnie. Taking things personally is what we do when we allow others to hurt us or let us down. We must use empathy to try to understand them and try to determine where they are coming from.

You feel hurt, but no one caused the feeling of hurt but you.

> Nobody can hurt me without my permission.
> —*Mahatma Gandhi*

Think of the next time someone cuts you off in traffic. Are you going to let it go with a smile or get angry and indicate with your hand that you're number one? I personally find it difficult to make such a sign with my paw, but through my many lives, I have not really found a need for it. Oh, I have on occasion arched my back and spit, but nowadays I find that I no longer need to do this. When you get angry and want to seek revenge, send love instead, for they don't understand the world or know what they are doing. Anger only hurts you, causes rash decisions, can make you look foolish, and detrimentally affects your health. Anger can destroy you as it takes over your life and distorts your perspective. Frankly, it's a waste of time. Don't let anger hinder your life. Has anger ever made you feel better? For me, a break always helps to put things back into perspective. Have a saucer of milk and relax. *Richard Carlson's* suggestion, "Don't sweat the small stuff," frankly is good advice. Just let it go and look forward.

People may not like you. Learn to live with it. We are not capable of befriending everyone. Just send them love and let it go. Why do some feel they must be liked by everyone? This is an impossible task. If you have a characteristic of someone who has wronged them, they will often transfer their dislike of that person to you. Surely at times you've had an instant dislike for someone, or even better, an instant fondness. Often you are unconsciously recognizing characteristics that you have yourself or that you have seen in others, or you are recognizing a soul you knew in a previous life. I have never met a mouse that I didn't like. A little salt and pepper … and there I go digressing again. But you get my point. It's great to be liked, but don't make that your goal. Doing what is right and kind will automatically attract people to you. Hey, and if you get a gentle pat on the head or a scratch behind the ear, all the better for you.

Whenever we take things personally, we have a sore spot too. What sore spot is the person touching when you feel hurt or let down? We should be constantly self-reflecting to try to understand our own pain and process the emotions attached to it. It may be that you have learned to be a people pleaser, and when you feel judged, it touches that sore spot that unless you are pleasing, you are not good enough. This is a learned behavior, and you have to understand where the trait is coming from (usually from our family of origin) and try to mitigate it. Life is about constant self-improvement, as we all have areas we can improve upon.

We should treat ourselves with tender, loving care. Never beat yourself up for making a mistake. Actually, there are no such things as mistakes, just learning experiences. Taking things personally, or beating yourself up, is a pointless exercise that just delays your personal growth. Remember, you are either acting in love or pain. The Beatles were right: "All You Need Is Love"!

The only person in this wide world that can make you happy or sad is you and you alone. In this drama we call life, it's all up to you. In reality, and fortunately for all of us, you must give people permission to hurt you. Do not give people the ability and power to hurt you. Have you experienced suffering, pain, and hurt? If someone tosses pain or hurt your way, toss it away. Don't accept it; return their message "undeliverable." We are all worthy. Don't let your ego allow others to harm you. The pain may arise from believing the negative words spoken about you. Self-reflect. If they turn out to be true, be grateful to them for alerting you to your error and concentrate on change. If, after self-reflection, you truly believe there is no truth to the allegation, brush it away and enjoy your day. Reward yourself with a saucer of milk, and if you don't want the saucer of milk, I would like to have first dibs!

Interestingly, often employees self-assess themselves harder than their supervisor's assessment. A great many of us feel that we are not strong enough or smart enough or beautiful enough. Your first step must be to accept yourself. Let your inner beauty show. Often, I have met people who may not exhibit the beauty of modern standards, but the goodness of their spirit and their genuine humanitarianism shine through, creating an outer beauty that overshadows those around them. We are all beautiful, but some of us just refuse to show it. Start loving yourself.

Fear knocked at the door. Love answered and no-one was there.
—*Wayne Dyer*

Find your inner peace by accepting others and forgiving those who may have hurt you, keeping in mind the hurt, is of your own creation. Let the past go. No matter how hard you try, you cannot change it. This may not happen overnight, but working toward peace of mind is worth the effort. It will come hurtling at you from within. Peace of mind brings with it tranquility, calmness, and the knowledge that you are a necessary part of this wonderful universe. Remove the negatives from your life and fill your inner being with the positives. Care not what people think or comment about you.

Live never to be ashamed if anything you do or say
is published around the world—
even if what is published is not true.
—*Richard Bach*, Illusions: The Adventures
of a Reluctant Messiah, p. 60

CHAPTER 8

Be Happy, Dance to the Beauty of the Day

Rule #5. Experience every day; each is like no other.

Lynnie and I liked to wander and experience this magical world whenever we had a chance. I of course was the one responsible for finding our way home. Lynnie was directionally challenged at the best of times and frequently was lost after her first step. Once she came up with the plan to leave bread crumbs as she walked in order find her way home and to impress me. She intentionally failed to inform me of this plan. As I tailed behind her this day, investigating anything unusual along our chosen path, I came across a bread crumb and, realizing my good fortune, ate it. This was my lucky day, I thought, as there seemed to be a lot of lost bread crumbs along our path. I made a mental note to walk this way more often. When it came time to head home, Lynnie was shocked, for the bread crumb trail had disappeared. She then informed me of her plan and asked me, "How could so much bread just disappear?" I pretended to look interested and searched with her for the elusive crumbs. Finally after wasting far too much time looking for what I knew was not to be found, I did the only honorable thing I could think of and blamed it on the birds.

Lynnie and I both enjoyed being near water. Notice I said *near* water, not in it. I did not like to get wet, as it matted my hair and made me look small. When it did happen, Lynnie would laugh and say I was having a bad hair day. But rain or shine, we experienced life, the sheer joy of the sun radiating down on us and the images of clouds as they danced with the wind across the skies. We enjoyed God's canvas, we watched, and we learned. I learned not to eat butterflies or fireflies. I have always wondered, as I am sure you have, why aren't there wild cookies roaming the countryside? Now I need a short break. I'm hungry.

> Life is not about waiting for the storm to pass,
> it's about learning to dance in the rain.
> —*Vivian Greene*

For Lynnie, dancing in the rain was easy. She had wellingtons. It's okay to dance under a tree though, providing there is no lightning. For some inexplicable reason, when Lynnie walks in the rain, I swear it appears to divide and fall heavier on either side of her. She just doesn't seem to get very wet. However, yours truly, who usually walks beside her, gets overly wet. To me, this is grossly unfair. After all, we are partners, and partners don't let partners get wet. I don't like bad hair days. Lynnie once bought me an umbrella hat, which is great if you are human and walk upright. When you walk on all fours, the umbrella hat only protects your head from getting wet. Meanwhile, my rear end gets soaked, and that is very uncomfortable. Does the rain really part? As I mentioned before, if you truly believe in something, it will happen. If you believe you will get a great parking space at the mall, you will. Just believe. If you believe you can't dance, you can't.

Speaking of dancing, I once caught a tap-dancing act years ago in a previous life. I was mesmerized watching the feet move so fast in a choreographed blur and hearing the soothing rhythmic tap, tap, tap of the shoes. It was music to my furry ears. I had to learn to tap dance. It was my calling. I needn't tell you, my size in tap shoes was not to be found. I discovered that by extending my claws and finding an appropriate surface, I could tap dance, or a close proximity to it. I found that a tin surface was best suited for me, and I spent many pleasurable hours tapping away. I was a dancing fool, and I was great. My best venue was on a tin roof where one day I was spotted, and to my pleasure a crowd gathered to watch. I danced my heart out. Rather than applause, people just stared in wonder and thought the roof was hot and burning my feet, causing me to quickly move them about. I don't need to tell you, I was mortified. As an aside, this is where the expression "Cat on a hot tin roof" arose. To this day, I am humiliated. Sometimes, even though it may be difficult, you just have to let go, and the important thing was I had a great time.

TVs, videos, electronic games, and so on are great for passing the time. People often comment, "I'm just killing time." Why would you want to do that? Children used to spend hours outside, their imaginations in high gear with their young minds absorbing infinite knowledge. Killing endless fake zombies on a screen cannot surpass the feeling and warmth of a light summer breeze or the beauty of the sun retreating beyond the horizon or walking in a misty morning on the moors. Beauty lies all around us. Beauty that far exceeds an exploding zombie head. Children today are being deprived of their birthright by our not helping them to see the beauty that surrounds them.

There is beauty everywhere. You just have to open your eyes.

—Frankie

Have you ever been down, depressed, lost in your self-created world of negativity and then spotted a monarch butterfly or a ruby-throated hummingbird? As you watched their apparent carefree, graceful motions as they went about their daily chores, their positive beauty overwhelmed your negativity, and for a brief moment you were free too. Your worries faded quietly from your mind as you absorbed the beauty before you. Nature in many ways acts as a neutralizing agent for our trials and tribulations. The beauty of the moment overwhelms our worries, casting them aside, unfortunately often only momentarily.

The greatest experience one can receive I wouldn't wish on anyone. A person I once knew was erroneously told he had only a short time to live. At first, depression set in as he realized that he would never again see a snowflake or know who won the FA Cup or the World Series. Previously he had hated winter, and now he yearned for the return of the winter season, the glistening icicles melting in the promising warmth of a spring day. What he had once disliked he now yearned for.

> Everything has beauty, but not everyone can see.
> —*Confucius*

He decided to live his life in full and enjoy every remaining minute of his visit here on earth. After a month of excessive spending, he found out his diagnosis, although correct for the symptoms he exhibited, was untrue. From that day forth, his old thought process was eradicated, and he appreciated and grew in awe of the wonders that surrounded him. He now lives each day loving the warmth of the sunshine, the majesty of a summer storm, the beauty of a rainbow or freshly fallen snow, and the love that animals exhibit for their offspring. Revel in your days. They are not many, and they are indeed precious. Life's visits are fleeting, and soon it will be time to return home. William James, one of America's most noted psychologists as well as philosopher, physician, and Harvard professor, refers to individuals who have had a major, possibly life-ending crisis as "twice-borns." They have gone through pain and mental suffering that has led them to rethink life and search for real meaning. Twice-borns then go on to a higher level of consciousness and seek their purpose in life, its true meaning, so to speak. So out of potential personal disaster comes greater happiness.

> Believe that life is worth living,
> and your very belief will help create the fact.
> —*William James*, *Pragmatism and Other Writings*, p. 240

In other words, James felt that happiness involves choice. How would you prefer to fill your inner being, with drugs, food or drink, or happiness? If you were given a few months to live, wouldn't your priorities change dramatically? Would the little things that bother you today still be of concern to you? To truly enjoy life, live each day as if it's your last.

It's only when we truly know and understand
that we have a limited time on earth
—and that we have no way of knowing when our time is up
—that we will begin to live each day to the fullest,
as if it was the only one we had.
—*Elisabeth Kubler-Ross*

The trick is to enjoy life. Don't wish away
your days, waiting for better ones ahead.
—*Marjorie Pay Hinckley*

One day your life will flash before your eyes.
Make sure it's worth watching.
—*Gerard Way*

You life is a book. The conclusion of each day finishes another chapter in your life. Each new morning commences your next chapter. Endeavor to make each new chapter something even you would be interested in reading. Make your life the great classic novel, not a comic book.

Each morning we are born again.
What we do today is what matters most.
—*Buddha*

Chapter 9
Believe

Rule #6. Believe in yourself and who you are.

If you don't believe in yourself and who you are, can you expect someone else to? I always told Lynnie her future was bright. After all, we had planned it together prior to leaving home. Sure there are no guarantees how life will unfold, but you have to believe. You are special because you are here. You are here for a purpose.

> When you doubt your power, you give power to your doubt.
> —*Honore de Balzac*

Far too many statements and feelings about ourselves are negative. Successful people believe in themselves. Perhaps that is the core to success.

> If you hear a voice within you say 'you cannot
> paint,' then by all means paint,
> and that voice will be silenced.
> —*Vincent van Gogh*

Lynnie was having a particularly tough night trying to do some math homework. She kept saying, "I'm stupid. I just can't do math."

I reminded her of Henry Ford's saying, "If you believe you can, or you believe you can't, you are absolutely right." As the exasperation began to mount, I gently distracted her. A break was what she needed at this time.

She was full of self-doubt and had blocked her mind to any new potential. I told her all humans have the same brain capacity. Some have natural tendencies in certain areas, just like either being left or right handed. Just because it is not a natural tendency does not mean there isn't ability there to tap into. It just takes a little more fortitude and patience. We all have different strengths and weaknesses. Lynnie, for instance, couldn't catch a mouse if her life depended on it. Personally, I found this quite sad. After some frolicking to clear the cobwebs, Lynnie went back to her math homework with fresh insight. I don't know how she did in that assignment, but at least she went back to it with renewed vigor and belief in her potential.

You are here to make a difference. You are not an accident that happened. You are part of this wonderful universe—a cog in the wheel of life.

> So that while we may be the protagonists
> of our own lives, we are the extras
> or spear carriers in some larger drama.
>
> —*Carl Jung*

I once met a dog who lived in his past. He had been a real scrapper. I heard that he had once been a champion fighter. He told me he used to be a boxer. Corny I know, but I can't help myself. I don't normally admit this, but there is a soft spot in my heart for dogs. You only tease the ones you love. They too have a role to play in this wondrous world. Don't live in your past. You are in the present for a reason, or you wouldn't be here. Forget past failures. They weren't failures but the building blocks of your future, just the same as your past successes. Don't be afraid to give your opinion; you won't if you truly believe in yourself.

Students in class often resist giving an answer for fear of being wrong. How sad, to refuse to share your creative thoughts because you might be wrong. We'd be still living in the dark ages if Edison had felt that way. Your participation and the exercising of your viewpoint in class is part of who you are becoming, the now you. You are part of the Supreme Being, and by Supreme Being, I am not referring to a lion. Certainly, if a lion spoke to me, I would listen, but I believe we all would. There are some people you just don't fool with.

I mentioned before how successful people knew they would be successful. They believed in themselves. Success is within you too. Think about it. If I can learn to tap dance, is your challenge so great? Self-doubt is very common, but why? An acquaintance applied for a job and was extremely honest in the interview. When asked if he could do some tasks, he responded that he wasn't proficient in that area. After he was offered the position, which he accepted, the senior interviewer took him aside and told him, "Whenever you are asked a question in an interview, state that you can do it, then leave and find out how to do it. Show confidence in yourself and know that you will succeed." The interviewer had once, during an interview, stated that he was proficient in financial reports, of which he knew nothing, and secured the job. After the interview, he studied everything he could find on corporate finances and was successful in mastering the subject. More importantly, he became the CEO of one of the largest and most successful companies in Canada. If you don't believe in yourself, why should anyone else? Would I have written this book if I didn't believe I could? Don't forget, I don't have opposable thumbs. I believe that my next meal is zooming toward me as we speak. I believe that I will receive several pats on the head today. I believe that there is a vacant, warm lap just around the corner, and I believe in me.

When you believe in yourself,
you have 100 percent of the people you need on your side.
—*Anima Vitam*

The more you believe in your own ability to succeed,
the more likely it is that you will.
—*Shawn Achor*

Unfortunately, some people feel that they have no value to anyone, that no one will miss them if they were gone. This is sad. You are just as important to the universe as I am or anyone else is. We all have special gifts, which are sometimes hard to discover, but they are there. You can achieve so much if you only believe in you. Salespersons often use positive affirmations such as a Post-it on the fridge to remind them each morning that they are a great salesperson. They believe, and they accomplish.

Failure to believe in yourself will surely hinder your progress. Avoid thoughts of negativity and secure your bright future. Family support, especially for children, can be very important. My current mother always encouraged me to be the best philosophical cat that I could be, giving me all the confidence I needed to go forward. Negative thoughts will derail you and only aid in you achieving less. Self-doubt is your enemy.

Some people look for reasons to fail; successful people don't. Don't let fear rule your future. Fear approaches us in many forms—financial insecurity, fear of being unloved, fear of the unknown, fear of our past returning, and I could go on, but you get the idea. Once again, I am happy to say you have the choice. Embrace the fear and nullify it or send it away. Enjoy your day or suffer. It's all up to you. For that we should all be very grateful.

If thou canst believe, all things are possible to him that believeth.
—*Mark* 9:23

CHAPTER 10
Judge Not

R ULE #7. NEVER JUDGE others.

Lynnie once queried, "How do you know who to trust or like?" Once again, we had found ourselves lying on a grassy hillside, watching the clouds drifting lazily by on their way to provide shade or rain where it was needed. We loved to see clouds in various shapes and sizes. Lynnie would see ships, cars, aunties, soccer balls, and the like. I, on the other hand, saw saucers of milk, mice dipped in butter, fish stuffed with crab, and various other snacks. I almost forgot shoes. Frequently we discussed the Bible and religion. Funny, I don't remember seeing biblical images in the clouds. In a sense, clouds are just clouds, bits of water vapor that have decided to have a get-together and set out to see the world. In reality, we see in them what we are looking for. Hopefully you will see beauty as we did.

As Wayne Dyer stated so eloquently, "When you judge another, you do not define them, you define yourself."

I believe one of the most important words in the English language is "empathy." We need it in all interactions, and if everyone used it in all communications, the world would be a more peaceful and tranquil place to live. This came to light one day when Lynnie was playing soccer in the park across from her home. She often went there with her soccer ball (remember our first meeting), and if there were enough children present, they would have a makeshift soccer game. This one day there was a group of boys a little older than Lynnie, and they were picking sides. Lynnie stood there and was the last one standing, but since it was her soccer ball, she was finally chosen. Not only was she a girl, but she was also small for her age. The boys were in for a rude awakening when they found Lynnie's skills to be far superior to theirs and she scored a number of goals against them. When we were walking home, Lynnie was quite pumped, her face glistening with perspiration and a scuffed ball tucked underneath her arm. She skipped along, and I said, "They judged you, didn't they? You know what they say: you can't judge a book by its cover!" Lynnie just smiled, as she knew what I meant and was happy to show the boys that lesson firsthand.

Your goal in life is not to be superior, just to be the best you can be. Never be catty. I personally find this term offensive. Where do people come up with these terms? To be catty is to be deliberately hurtful. Cats just don't do that, nor do we ignore you. When you call a dog, he comes running. With cats, we are just not the same. It's not that we don't want to obey; we're just different, independent. We'll look at you acknowledging that we heard your request, and we'll let you know.

When feeling the need to judge others, just don't. How are you helping? Surely, you can't presuppose that you are aware of all the causations of their actions.

Before you criticize someone,
you should walk a mile in their shoes.
That way when you criticize them,
you are a mile away from them and you have their shoes.
—*Jack Handey*

—

Develop empathy, which will help. Do you ever feel that you are being helped when people openly criticize you? Which is easier, criticizing or showing empathy? Respond with empathy, compassion, and understanding. Do you believe anger will help? Sometimes we judge too quickly. It's natural to us. I try to reserve judgment on dogs before I declare them totally insane.

Do we judge because we are insecure? Has judging others become a habit? Do you judge to be part of group criticism? Is it caused by jealousy? Do we judge to build our own ego? Judging others will not make you a more joyous person or one that I would choose to be around. Does criticizing others improve your lifestyle or help you in any way? On the other hand, judgments can hurt people or result in stereotyping. Frankly, I don't see the point in judging others. I have not had their myriad of experiences, I don't know all the facts, and I can't say how I would react in their shoes. Plus, in most instances, I don't think they would fit. I'm sure that we do not like to be judged critically. The old adage, treat others the way you would like to be treated, certainly is appropriate here.

Long ago, I used to often judge people on their appearance, and often I was wrong. Being judgmental can cause all kinds of problems. What if Jesus reappeared in beggar's clothing? Would you reject him based on the way he was dressed or would you treat him with human respect and recognize him as a fellow traveler of equal status?

It's not what you look at that matters, it's what you see.
—*Henry David Thoreau*

It's true: 'Everybody is a genius. But if
you judge a fish by its ability to
climb a tree, it will live its whole life believing that it is stupid.'"
—*Albert Einstein*

—

Give people a chance to influence you before jumping to conclusions. I'm a tap-dancing philosopher, but some people see only a cat. I'm so much more than just a cat, although a cat is a fine thing to be. We often judge people out of habit, and we can consciously stop it. We really do not know what causes people's behavior or reactions to us. Give them the benefit of the doubt. The reasons for their behavior might be deemed legitimate if you were aware of them. If you judge people incorrectly on incomplete information, then you will treat them incorrectly, and that would be a shame. If you are unaware of the full story, how can you be judgmental? Also be careful not to judge others based on opinions from those around you. Their opinions may or may not be correct and sometimes are based on erroneous assumptions. Always keep in mind, no one is perfect, not even me, and we are all different, with different beliefs and ways of doing things.

It is worth repeating:

> When you judge another, you do not define them.
> You define yourself.
> —*Wayne Dyer*

CHAPTER 11

The Joy of Differences

R ULE # 8. REJOICE in differences.

I once introduced Lynnie to a friend of mine. She was a three-legged albino cat who was a little hard of hearing. Her name was Lucky. Lucky always appeared embarrassed due to her differences, but it was her uniqueness that made her so beautiful. Lynnie first met Lucky in the same Manchester park where we reunited a few years previously. At first, Lynnie was taken aback as I introduced Lucky to her, for she had not met this cat. Lucky then limped forward all the while looking directly up into Lynnie's eyes with her beautifully large, round pink eyes and purring tentatively as she neared. Lucky had heard about Lynnie and had already found a place for Lynnie in her heart. Fearing rejection as she had experienced so many times before, Lucky crouched a little on her two fore paws as if in a subservient bow, all the while carefully gazing into Lynnie's eyes. Lynnie gave a small squeal of delight and gathered Lucky up into her arms. Lynnie only saw the beauty, and Lucky only saw a new best friend. Lynnie immediately named her Angel, and Angel purred in agreement. Angel, the cat formerly known as Lucky, felt cherished for the first time.

Lynnie enjoyed learning about different cultures. Her parents were brought up in colonial India, and that culture had always fascinated her. I proudly watched as she learned more and more about the differences in people, their beliefs, customs, and way of doing things. I knew that the appreciation of other cultures wasn't always the norm and hoped that her generation would be more open and accepting than previous ones.

Think how dull this world would be if we were all the same.

> No-one is born hating another person
> because of the color of his skin, or his background,
> or his religion. People must learn to hate,
> and if they can learn to hate,
> they can be taught to love,
> for love comes more naturally to the
> human heart than its opposite.
> —*Nelson Mandela*

> If two people agree on everything, one of them is unnecessary.
> —*Unknown*

Did you ever notice how differences appear to divide us? Why is that? If you are different from me, should I be offended? I am actually curious, and as far as I know, curiosity did not kill this cat. I once spent a lifetime in India. This culture was totally different from any other I had experienced. Sure there was poverty, but there was also a great deal of generosity that was not government mandated; it was generosity freely given from the heart. In many ways, I loved the Hindu philosophy, which had no need to convert. They could accept that you were different or had different beliefs. Everything was alien to me, spiritual beliefs, language, clothing, food, tradition, and so on. Their clothing exhibited the most beautiful, vibrant colors I had ever seen. I even became a kaleidoscope of brilliant colors at India's Holi Festival of Colors. Some people say cats can't see color, but I can see it just fine, and I like it. I always want to learn more about different cultures, how they live, how they function, and what they believe. Life is about learning, and who to better learn from than someone who doesn't have a similar background to you.

Studies have indicated that teams with diverse backgrounds are more difficult to manage but are also much more creative and hence valuable to an organization. A lawyer I once knew always liked working with lawyers from different countries because they brought different insight and approaches to international cases. Sometimes I think people fear differences, and that causes their hostility. I've never been able to figure out what there is to fear. In many ways, we are all just people, or cats, and we are all unique beings, and hence the differences. We all have a special talent, and we are all here for a purpose. It took me a couple of lifetimes to discover mine. Some beings are just more different, and that is to me very special. Would it really be better if we were all just clones? What a boring world that would be. Embrace the world's differences.

Acceptance of others, their looks, their behaviors,
their beliefs, brings you an inner peace and tranquility,
instead of anger and resentment.
—*Unknown*

In *The Giver* by Lois Lowry, sameness is valued above diversity, and is that not also what George Orwell's *1984* is all about? Do these societies appeal to you? If so, I grieve for you. We are all here to learn, and a closed mind is a waste. Seeing the world from different perspectives is the joy of living. Like it or not, we are now living in a global economy, and interaction with different cultures is inevitable as our communities are also becoming more diverse. Maybe instead of looking for differences, we can look for similarities. There are always a lot of these as well. After all, most differences are in reality minor. None of us are travelling the only true path. Indeed, we are all the same in that we are all different.

> A fruit salad is delicious precisely because
> each fruit maintains its own flavor.
> —*Sean Covey*, *The 7 Habits of Highly Effective Teens*

> It's never the differences between people that surprises us.
> It's the things that, against all odds, we have in common.
> —*Jodi Picoult*, *House Rules*

> All the events of your past have formed a lens, or paradigm,
> through which you see the world.
> And since no-one's past is exactly like
> anyone else's, no two people see alike.
> —*Sean Covey*, *The 7 Habits of Highly Effective Teens*

CHAPTER 12
Fear Not

Rule # 9. Never fear the future; embrace it and be happy.

Chronophobia describes the phobia of fear of the future and passing time. People can fear the future for many reasons. As we age and our mortality in this lifetime begins to dawn on us, some fear the inevitability of death. Death in this lifetime is not an end. We return home and in due course are reborn. Consider it a long voyage, although some return to this plane very quickly. To fear the future would imply that we only have one future, and that just isn't so, for we have many futures.

> He that fears not the future may enjoy the present.
> —*Thomas Fuller*

> He who fears he shall suffer already suffers what he fears.
> —*Michel de Montaigne*

> I am not afraid of tomorrow,
> for I have seen yesterday and I love today.
> —*William Allen White*

> There is no such thing as a problem without a gift for you
> in its hands. You seek problems because you need their gifts.
> **Richard Bach**, *Illusions: The Adventures of a Reluctant Messiah*, p. 71

On an early autumn day, with winter peeking around the corner and the greenery turning into a myriad of brilliant colors, Lynnie seemed not to be enjoying the spectacle and mentioned that she was troubled. This surprised me as I was basking in the last of summer's warmth and the beauty of the fall foliage. Lynnie was always such a positive happy soul at home or here on earth. Lynnie's soft brown, worrisome eyes revealed her inner concerns. She explained that she had forgotten to put her books and pens away prior to leaving her school classroom. Her teacher, whom she adored, might be upset with her, and she was concerned that she had let her down. This small problem weighed heavily on a young girl's mind. To her, this trivial matter by world standards was important, very important. At the time, it became very important to me as well. After all, we were the Three Mouseketeers. I will stop here to say that this is not a spelling mistake or a failure to count properly. The name was our joke, as I liked mice and we considered Angel as the third companion. As we age, we learn what matters most in life. Years later, we recalled the incident and laughed at the unimportance of it all and our needless worry. Life is full of little worries; stress the word *little* and keep them where they belong, in the back recesses of your mind. Worrying never solves a problem. Generally, it increases your anxiety and makes matters worse and smothers your happiness. How often have you fretted over a possible future event only to later realize that you had worried needlessly? Put things in perspective and live your life to its fullest each and every day. Be the best you can be. Happiness is a choice that you make. Make the right choice.

Live in the present, remember the past,
and fear not the future,
for it doesn't exist and never shall.
There is only now.
—*Christopher Paolini*

One is never afraid of the unknown;
one is afraid of the known coming to an end.
—*Jiddu Krishnamurti*

You really have to love the beauty and charm of this world. Sure there are some flaws. Snow can become water, not something I'm particularly fond of. Wet fur just doesn't sit well with me or on me, but that doesn't mean snow can't be fun. For example, in medieval times, I used to walk in the snow and drag my tail. People thought the impression in the snow must have been the result of a giant rat stalking them. The only thing worse than a rat is a giant rat. People felt better to have me afoot, and it often led to an extra saucer of milk. After all, I would need my strength to take on such a formidable foe. Between you and me, if there had really been a giant rat, I was not going to seek it out let alone fight it. A few days would pass without tracks, and it was assumed that it had been vanquished and yours truly was a hero. I used to laugh myself to sleep. Ethically it may not have been right, but it didn't hurt anyone, and it amused me, and I like to be amused. The real fun would have occurred if I had secured tiny shoes and picked up my tail. Their imaginations would have run wild. Perhaps an evil elf had passed by. With two sets of prints, one where I dragged my tail, it could have been an evil elf riding a giant rat. Humans are funny. They will time and again think the worst.

When Lynnie and I were sitting pondering the beauty of nature, she would often say, "I wonder where I will be in five years." She had a hope for the future and couldn't wait to be of an age when she had

—

some control over her life. If only we could all feel the same way. The future is ours to embrace. It hurtles relentlessly toward us with lessons, gifts, and happiness if we choose to seize it. Acceptance is your choice.

We frequently worry about things that never actually happen or affect us. Often when children hear a noise in the night, they immediately know it's a monster on the prowl. Cherish the child who thinks in July that Santa Claus has arrived early and with loads of presents. We choose whether we are happy or sad. Often I have witnessed people who have suffered untold hurts, and they smile as if the sun shone exclusively for them. Count how often in a day you think negative thoughts and positive thoughts. You may be surprised how many more negative thoughts you have versus positive. If you are always negative and feel that the world is against you, then that will be your lot in life. The Bobby McFerrin song "Don't Worry Be Happy" might just be the philosophy for you.

> When I was five years old, my mother always told me
> that happiness was the key to life.
> When I went to school, they asked me what I wanted to be
> when I grew up. I wrote down "Happy."
> They told me I didn't understand the assignment,
> and I told them they didn't understand life.
> —*John Lennon*

It bewilders me why people can't just be happy. If you constantly tell your mind that you are unhappy, it will be a self-fulfilling prophecy, and the universe will provide you with sadness. Be careful what you wish for. Once I ran into a professor who began to talk to me. I am sure that many of you converse with your pets. I like to tilt my head so people know I understand and can follow the conversation. I learned this trick from other humans. Tilt the head and everything is okee-doe-kee. Anyway, he told me of a student in his university class that looked very worried and dejected. He approached the student and asked if everything was okay. She responded that everything was going wrong, life was terrible. The professor told her that in the not too distant future, she would look back at these years as the best years in her life. She quickly and dejectedly responded, "You mean it's going to get worse?"

I've never understood why people try to escape life by taking drugs. Now I'm not a saint. I have dabbled in catnip, and I'm not going to claim, as a certain politician did, that I didn't inhale. In my progression of lives, I've made mistakes. It was part of my process, and like Edison, I learned from my mistakes. So learn to choose happy. Is there really any other option? Tell yourself every morning that you are happy, and soon it will become your reality. How fortunate for us that the happiness we strive for is already here within us. We already possess the keys to happiness, success, and even our good health.

You may not be the sole author of your creation. Others may have helped you move toward your rebirth. However, you are the sole author of your journey in this world. Isn't it about time you enjoyed it?

> No matter how bad you feel at day's end,
> just beyond that beautiful sunset,
> a whole new day is dawning just for you.
> —*Frankie*

Happiness is an experience of your unconditioned
self without the burden of
"must," "ought" or "should."
—*Robert Holden*

Happiness is your original nature, it is what you first experienced
before you began to identify with a body, a nationality, some
school grades, a family role, the story of you, your business card,
your social security number, and other mistaken identities.
—*Robert Holden*

Whether you want to see the future or not, it is on its way. The future is tomorrow's today. Don't fear it; embrace it. The fact that you have a future is the greatest gift imaginable. Some don't receive this gift with all of its opportunities. Your future is based on the decisions and vision you have today. Not all decisions will be stellar, but each decision will lead you down the path to today. I have had numerous trials and tribulations in my lives, but they have brought me to today, and I look forward to my future.

When events bother you and cause you to worry, they do so because you allow them to take over your emotions and hence your very life. I'm not saying that you shouldn't worry if behind you is a ten-foot brick wall, and a pack of angry dogs lacking in a sense of humor in front of you. That is a natural fight-or-flight reaction that helps us survive. What I'm saying is that there are a lot of events that we worry and fret about that never really cause us harm. Even if there was harm, worrying did not in any way alleviate the situation. Stress can affect you in numerous ways, including weakening the immune system. We all know stress is not good for us, so stop worrying and do something about the situation at hand. If nothing further can be done at the moment, do something else productive or enjoy yourself. Life can be good if you let it. It is up to you to determine your level of happiness. The way you view your world is your choice. I for one prefer to live in a happy world. Look, if you dig deep enough, even a puppy is kind of cute.

There are strangers in your future. If you meet a stranger, why not welcome him or her? There are many tell-tale signs that indicate their nervousness. Alleviate them of that. Open a door for someone, and although I personally find that very difficult, it can make a person's day. I used to tap dance for people, but it tended to frighten them, not the effect I wanted at all. One person had the nerve to shout, "Mad cat!" I don't do that anymore. Fine artistic expression is often not fully appreciated.

Be happy and don't let other people or fears of the yet unknown try to take your happiness away from you. Be proud about what you bring to the interaction. Live in the world of your choosing, not theirs. People who are unkind to you have an issue, not you.

The future is going to surprise you, but isn't that what you really desire? How boring it would be if the future was foretold and there were no surprises, not unlike watching a movie you've already seen. If you liked the movie, by all means enjoy the memories, but no one wants to see the same movie every day.

> The future started yesterday, and we're already late.
> —*John Legend*

I believe in laughter, I believe in kindness, I believe that the world is good and we can make it better, and I believe in you. Now march boldly into your future and, above all, enjoy it.

CHAPTER 13

Peace and Tranquility

R ULE #10: It is important to search out peace and tranquility.

Lynnie and I used to talk about wealth and if that should be a goal in life. Would wealth actually make you happier? Does money relate to happiness? I asked Lynnie if she was happy even with a family life where money was not plentiful and where there were a lot of siblings that needed to share it? What did she feel was lacking, if anything? Lynnie paused for several long seconds. She had love. She had friendship, and not just me, for she was loved by many. Perhaps even more important, she had laughter. Realizing this, she exclaimed, "I am rich beyond my wildest hopes and dreams," and that she was. Her thoughts moved me and caused a tear in my eye, although it might have been gas.

Materialism is often just a distraction; after all, you're not taking it with you. I know. I tried once but failed. When your time comes and it is time to return home, your last thought is not about banking or an investment; it is about the love and experience you shared. My companionship with Lynnie was a wonderful time. She was so eager to learn and could easily transcend to new ideas, gently leaping over previously taught principles. Without a multitude of possessions or wealth, she knew in her subconscious peace and tranquility were to be hers.

One thing Lynnie and I would always do is stop and smell the roses. On our endless walks together, we viewed the world with awe, appreciation, and inspiration. Lynnie loved nothing more than going for a Sunday drive through the country. She could sit in the car for hours and be quite content looking at the rolling hills, stone walls, wildflowers, and animals. Whenever she would get stressed or lose focus and become agitated, I would remind her of these times. I had taught her to bring those scenes to her mind's eye early in our work together. It was what psychotherapists call your "safe place." It worked beautifully to calm Lynnie down or bring her back to rationalization if she allowed herself to go on a journey of catastrophizing. I would at this time like to point out the improper use of the word *cat* in the previous sentence. We are positive creatures. I have yet to hear of dogastrophizing. This is probably William Shakespeare's fault.

But it is even more important to provide peace and tranquility to others, and it will bounce back your way. I once saved a little wounded bird and cared for it until a human took it away from me. Truthfully, I was actually saving it for dinner. Nonetheless, I got credit for helping the bird, and although credit does not fill one's stomach, it did feel good. There has been a lot of talk about bullying in schools, but why is it so prevalent? Why does a dog want to chase me when he has never met me and knows nothing about me?

There's only one reason why you're not experiencing bliss at this present moment, and it's because you're thinking or focusing on what you don't have ... but, right now you have everything you need to be in bliss.
—*Anthony de Mello*

We make a living by what we get,
but we make a life by what we give.
—*Winston Churchill*

Poisonous people are not allowed to take my peace. It's difficult
sometimes but I can't take on other people's negativity.
—*Alex Elle*

Speak when you are angry—and you'll make
the best speech you'll ever regret.
—*Laurence J. Peter*

Our own worst enemy cannot harm us
as much as our unwise thoughts.
—*Buddha*

In your lifetime, you are going to meet a lot of people that just irk
you. I've talked about toxic people, but these aren't toxic people,
and they really aren't there to intentionally annoy you or cause you
trouble, even though they may. For lack of a better descriptive term,
these are people who have chosen the path of lesser intelligence,
or the logically impaired. You remember the line from *Sixth Sense*
where a psychic, Cole Sear, tells psychologist Malcolm Crowe, "I
see dead people. They don't even know they're dead." I once saw a
spin-off poster that read, "I see dumb people ... they're everywhere.
They walk around like everyone else and they don't even know
they're dumb."

Truly stupid people will never know they are stupid.
—*John Cleese*

The world is full of such people. They could be less developed souls
or souls that have returned to earth to learn within the restrictions
and limitations they have placed upon themselves, or their task in

—
77

life might be to teach us tolerance. Remember, although they may be a bother to you, their life is not without the problems that ride alongside a life of limited intelligence. It is not a bed of roses for them either. They may, despite their limitations, have a better job or greater success than you, but remember that is their journey, not yours, and their life is their road to travel. Help them if you are capable but don't expect everyone to react to situations as you do. Bless them, for they have chosen a rockier road to travel.

Individuals who are common-sense impaired can be frustrating, but they can also be very loving. They will learn their life lessons as their journey progresses, but there is a very strong likelihood that you have met them for a reason. We do not have chance encounters. We meet souls that we have met before in other lifetimes. There are likely issues to be resolved, or perhaps they are there to offer support, not unlike me being here for Lynnie. As I have travelled through my many lifetimes, I have encountered Lynnie numerous times. Sometimes the gaps between our meetings have been lengthy, other times very short. We've always planned our visits to this plane. I can't help but recall Vera Lynn's beautiful ballad, "We'll Meet Again," whenever it comes for Lynnie and I to part. When we part, we know that parting is temporary, as we meet again at home.

Returning home can be really scary for some individuals. At first it can be a shock. Think of it merely as a transition. Imagine the butterfly. The larva or caterpillar goes into a deep sleep as a chrysalis to undergo metamorphosis and emerge as a beautiful butterfly. As a chrysalis, the soon-to-be butterfly must feel its life is over, and yet it has only just begun. We too go through stages not unlike the butterfly. We go through metamorphosis in order to return home prior to returning here again.

One of our worst enemies is our thoughts. Yes, we can have wonderful thoughts and need thinking to plan our day, solve problems, and so on. However, I think we can all relate to the racing thoughts that come to us day in and day out. Worrying about something at work, relationships, children, what we are having for supper, and so on. If worry solved anything, then I would say go right ahead. Unfortunately, worry never solved anything, changed anything, or improved a situation. It just makes it worse. So we need to learn to control those thoughts. And, yes, we can control those thoughts. The brain is our tool, and we can use it however we want. So take control, chase those worries away, and refuse to be weighed down with life's trivialities. They may not seem like trivialities at the time, but trust me, they are. In the grand scheme of things, the relationship, the work stress, and yes, even what is for dinner are trivial. Wayne Dyer wrote a book called *Change Your Thoughts, Change Your Life*. In fact, many things have been written about how your thoughts can change your course in life. So if this is the case, change your thoughts to peaceful, tranquil ones.

Easy for you to say, I am hearing … we cats have extremely good hearing. It isn't as hard as you think. Deep breathing can help us slow things down and give us the time to take control. Meditation can also help us to quiet the mind. Relaxation strategies or just doing something we love takes back the control of the thoughts. In essence, we just have to retrain the brain. Let it know who the boss is! Once you slow down the thoughts, banish negative thinking, and reframe into positive thoughts, you will find peace and tranquility are not far behind. Try it … I think you will like it.

A baby leaving its warm, quiet home to be born truly must feel that the end is near as it bursts forth into bright light, cooler temperatures, loud noise, and gets slapped, and yet their earthly journey has just begun. At that stage, they remember home as a beautiful place, a place of peace, equality, and learning, where all of our differences vanish. Once we return home, we are always joyous at our presence there. It is a respite prior to returning to this plane. We work with our partners and friends on self-improvement, and we plan our next visitation to earth, much as one would plan a vacation but in a little more detail.

I'm off to find a sunny windowsill to meditate right now. If you can't find a windowsill big enough for you, go take a hot bath or leisurely walk and think positively.

It is indeed a strange world, but none of us are strangers.

—*Frankie*

I don't like to call home an afterlife as many do. I prefer to refer to it as the in-between life. We return to this world over and over again, learning and improving through experiences, which to us are very real, but in reality our world is an illusion, much the same as watching a movie. You find yourself drawn in, involved, and the movie and our current visitation are as real as a tap-dancing cat, and, to reiterate, I am real. Now when you have reached perfection, you do not return but become a part of the greater cosmos. Now I'm sure you're asking yourself, how it is that I continue to return to earth? That question befuddles me as well. Perhaps it's just because I am here to educate. I mean really, how could you improve on me?

What is the meaning of life? If you are reading this, then you have meaning. Actually, if you aren't reading this, you still have meaning, but I think it would be more purrfect if you got to know me and helped me get some shoes. Seek out happiness and love. By love, I don't necessarily mean another person but learn to love yourself. It's nice to share your love of life with another person, a friend, or I particularly think a cat can be a great companion to share your life with. I am particularly fond of cats with boots. In my younger days, I had a fondness for Puss n Boots.

Ego says, "Once everything falls into place, I'll feel peace."
Spirit says, "Find your peace, and then
everything will fall into place."
—*Marianne Williamson*

May you find serenity and tranquility
in a world you may not always understand.
—*Sandra Sturtz*

Epilogue

Cats don't live as long as humans. Our spirits like to return home sooner than yours. It's not that we don't love to be with you, but as Dorothy would say, "There's no place like home." As time progressed, I grew a little grayer around the whiskers, my eyesight slowly grew dimmer, and the vibrant colors of this beautiful, beautiful world faded. My little girl was now fifteen, soon to be a young lady with new dreams and adventures. One night with dusk fast approaching, I had the uneasy feeling of pending doom, a feeling I have had many times before throughout the eons. A cool breeze carried Lynnie's melodious voice to my ears as she returned from a Manchester United soccer match. She had been gone for most of the afternoon, and I missed her dearly. You see, I loved this girl. She always made me laugh. We would chuckle for hours until our sides hurt. We were always happy together. Life was our catnip.

> A day without laughter is a day wasted.
> —*Nicolas Chamfort*

There was the hope that she might have a treat for me, as my hunting skills had declined. Birds no longer feared me, and I think sometimes the mice were laughing at me. I swear I heard one refer to me as Shorty. The sight of Lynnie made my heart fill with joy, and I ran across the road to be in her loving arms. The squeal of the breaks and a thud alerted me to my mistake, and I knew flying through the air was not natural. I lay against the curb as my life slowly ebbed away. I was going home. Lynnie scooped me up. I felt no pain. My back was broken. She put milk on my lips to try to revive me, but it was not to be. I could no longer swallow. My time was fast approaching. Our eyes met, and I said my goodbyes and thanked her for her kindness and for being such a good pupil. There was so much more that I wanted to tell her, my mind was clouded with so many unachieved expectations, but there really was no need: she would do great. I loved this woman-child, for she always forgave my imperfections.

> What greater gift than the love of a cat?
> —*Charles Dickens*

The world would be a better place with her in it. Lynnie sobbed, "Don't leave me, Kitty. Please don't go. I … I still need you, I love you, I'll fix you." Colors were starting to fade as the world transitioned to a fuzzy black and white. Her tears fell on my fur, and for once I didn't mind getting wet. One last purr, and it was my time to die, but as sure as the spring arrives and the daffodils bloom, I will return. I tried to tell her not to mourn me. She knew I would return, but the parting of old friends is hard on the emotions of a young girl.

> Don't cry or be sad over memories—
> memories are a wonderful thing to have.
> Cherish them.
> —*Frankie*

> You may not be solely responsible for your creation,
> but you are the sole planner of
> your journey in this world.
> It is time to enjoy it.
> —*Frankie*

I love the path that I have chosen to follow, and I hope you can find your path, the one that makes you happiest, as Lynnie has done. Our purpose here is not to accumulate wealth, shoes, or mice but to make the earth a better place than when we got here. Random acts of kindness create ripples like those on a pond and can cause effects that you may never have dreamed of. Looking down at my fur, the blood was gone, and my fur looked young and vibrant. The stars seemed brighter. As my spirit separated, I slipped from the comfort of her loving arms for one last time. I began to drift upward, reluctant and sad to go but anxious to return home. Do not mourn me, for I will be back and hopefully a bit taller. You see, I still have dreams yet to live.

Until We Rendezvous Once More

Words or poetry can no longer express my
spiritual love and ageless devotion to you.
Your happiness has become my happiness, and
your grief and sorrow are but my wounds.
In attempting to describe my devotion to you,
the multitude of words becomes so fragile
they flow as mere particles dispersed in the
winds. I have lived through your eyes and
viewed the world in ways I did not dream possible.
I need not be mourned, for I have
lived in the inspiration of your love. As my last
breath on this earth escapes, my last
image is that of you. Though I may be gone from
this earthly plane, I will always be with
you. In the night, I'll watch over you as you
gently sleep, invading your dreams to greet
you once again. In the dawn, as you walk,
the mist will be my tears of parting,

—

the wind on your cheek a fluttering kiss of
goodbye, the whispers in the trees
my promise to return. When your time has
come and darkness invades the corners
of your mind, you'll see me. For I'll be there
to greet you and to guide you along
our eternal journey.

—*Frankie*

Don't view me as vain, although I'm one cool cat. I just for once would like to be a bit taller. When I return, there will be a new vitality in my step, and my aches and pains will be a distant memory. So someday soon, I will return, and if you see a handsome kitten with loving eyes that appear to look within you to your very core, with a tail that goes straight up and is a bit tall for his age, that may be me. I will be here to help, so take me home and be sure to feed me. Being a guide can build up an appetite. I am partial to milk and fish, so keep some on hand just in case. Looking forward to meeting you soon.

I've seen the sun ascend to the heavens over the pyramids,
I have sipped brandy with Napoleon,
I have been turned into a kaleidoscope of brilliant
hues at India's Holi Festival of Colors,
I believe that the world is a truly wondrous place,
I believe in me, and I certainly believe in you.

—*Frankie*

Goodbye …

Frankie has left the planet … for now!

Appendix A

The Bible and Reincarnation

Prior to, during, and following Jesus's life, reincarnation was not only accepted by many but was supported by Christian leaders such as *Origen* (AD 185–254), who commented:

> The soul has neither beginning nor end.
> [They]come into this world strengthened by the victories
> or weakened by the defeats of their previous lives.

Reincarnation was not just a Christian theory. Native American cultures also believed in reincarnation, that life flows in a circular motion. Reincarnation in Hebrew is in fact *gilgul*, which means "turning in a circle." There is no dispute that the Bible has been edited over the years, but has it been edited correctly? Has Christianity strayed from its early beginnings? Is it about to be reborn?

In AD 553, the Second Council of Constantinople met and decided to remove reincarnation from Christian belief. Pope Vigilius did not attend the council even though present in Constantinople at the time. In the sixth century, the Roman state exercised a great deal of control over the Church, and reincarnation would not be helpful in establishing absolute control by the emperor. Rulers wanted people to sacrifice their lives for their emperor and church. Reward would come later in the afterlife. If you were out of line in this life, eternal damnation would be yours. A belief that there might be a second chance to correct current negative behavior in the next life would undermine the Church's or government's desire of absolute control. Keep in mind, changes to the Bible and Christian theology were not a mammoth task. Most people at the time either could not read, did not have access to scriptures, or were banned from reading the Bible. Against the will of the rulers, reincarnation really didn't stand a chance. As time progresses, scholars are rethinking the changes that the scriptures have undergone.

The Bible contains numerous passages alleged to refer to reincarnation. Jesus three times indicated that John was Elijah (Matthew 17:12–13, Matthew 11:13–14, Mark 9:13). It was even questioned who Jesus was.

> "Whom do men say that I the Son of man am?"
> —*Matthew* 16:13

The disciples responded;

> "Some say that thou art John the Baptist: some Elias;
> and others, Jeremias or one of the prophets."
> —*Matthew* 16:14

The disciples are speculating who Jesus was in a previous life. Jesus does not deny or reject reincarnation. While in Caesarea Philippi, Jesus asks his disciples:

> "Whom do men say that I am?"
> —*Mark* 8:27

> And they answered, "John the Baptist: but some say Elias;
> and others, One of the prophets."
> —*Mark* 8:28

Doesn't the question and answer suggest that reincarnation was an accepted philosophy? Note that they did not answer, "The son of Mary and Joseph," which would be the obvious. Jesus did not need to tell people that reincarnation was a fact since they already believed in it, as it appears to have been a widely accepted concept at the time. There were plenty of opportunities to refute the concept, but it appears that such comments were never made or recorded.

In Malachi 1:2–3 and Romans 9:11–13, it is said that Jacob was loved by God and Esau was hated prior to their birth. These passages certainly confirmed preexistence, which goes hand in hand, or as I would say, paw in paw, with reincarnation. *Jeremiah* 1:5 also talks of his preexistence.

> "Before I formed thee in the belly I knew thee;
> and before thou cameth forth out of the womb I sanctified thee,
> and I ordained thee a prophet unto the nations."

In John 9:2, Jesus and his disciples encounter a man born blind. The disciples question Jesus, asking, was this the result of sins of the parents or the man? A man being born blind due to previous sins certainly suggests a previous life or the very least preexistence. It appears that Jesus and his disciples understood this, and there is no evidence of disagreement. The account of this event clearly indicates that it was understood or believed that a baby could be born blind as a result of previous sin prior to birth.

Some in Christianity oppose the concept of reincarnation, seeing it as a conflict with resurrection. I personally don't see the conflict. Why can't resurrection be rebirth? We hear talk about "for all of eternity." I've been around for a long time, but I simply can't get my mind around this concept. To me, an eternity is the time between lunch and dinner. Lynnie strongly agrees with me on this. If God has granted us eternity, why are we granted only one hundred years or fewer here on earth to learn and to grow? Wouldn't reincarnation make more sense? Yet we can't remember past lives. Indeed most of us have difficulty remembering what has happened to us in this life.

Children often talk about previous lives or often exhibit skills beyond their years, such as a concert violinist at an extremely young age, often referred to as a natural prodigy. Our subconscious remembers, and past-life experience can sometimes be brought forward through hypnosis. It is rare that people are born with the memories of past lives, but it does happen. There is the extremely moving story of Jenny Cockell, an English woman who remembers a past life and eventually meets several of her children from that former life (*Across Time and Death*, Simon & Schuster Inc., 1994, ISBN 0-671-88986-9).

The Old Testament fails to refute reincarnation. *Job* 14:14 asks: "If a man die, shall he live again?"

No answer is forthcoming. In biblical times, the concept of reincarnation was so pervasive that there was no questioning of the concept. It can be argued that the Bible does not discuss many concepts, but that does not make them any less true, although, as already discussed, many have concluded that the Bible in its original text supported reincarnation.

Orthodox Jewish leaders around the time of Jesus taught the concept of reincarnation. Philo Judaeus, Hillel, and Jehoshuah ben Pandira, all illustrious names in Jewish religious chronicles, supported the concept. Plato was a proponent of reincarnation and taught that we came to earth to gain knowledge, knowledge that would require more than one lifetime to acquire. I like to think of our time on earth as being in school, time in between lives as our recess, a time to reflect on events, where we've been and where we are going and then to plan our future life. Earth is so much more than just one big litter box. We are provided with the opportunity to evolve again and again. Reincarnation is not only logical but provides us with a sense of justice and forgiveness. I, and only I, am responsible for my future evolution. The soul eventually evolves away from earthly belongings and becomes one with God. Those who die still yearning for the earth's riches will be afforded the opportunity of returning. Overcome evil, forsake earthly goods, and find love, and your schooling on earth will end, as you have graduated.

> Him that overcometh will I make a pillar
> in the temple of my God,
> and he shall go no more out ...
> —*Revelation* 3:12

About the Author

B ILL ANGUS HAS HAD a varied career in both the private and public sectors. He has been an international business executive, with over thirty years experience in strategic management, human resources management, labor relations, and law. Bill has also been a newspaper columnist and entertainment photographer. Bill is currently a university professor and TV and radio political talk show host. He has published a number of articles, presented numerous seminars on workplace issues and employment law, and has been a keynote speaker at various conferences. Bill specializes in creativity training, body language, and employee development and has demonstrated that creativity can be taught and developed. As a graduate of the Faculty of Law at Queen's University and a member of numerous professional associations, including the Ontario Bar, Bill brings a wealth of professional experience to his seminars.

Illustrations by:

Sam Oosterman lives in Victoria, B.C., with her family and dog, Seal. She is studying psychology and enjoys drawing, photography, and writing in her spare time.

Printed in the United States
By Bookmasters